Hear Us Roar

Unapologetic Women Leading In Corporate America

By Elizabeth Lions

Denise,
Best to you!
Elizabeth

*This book is dedicated to
Shankaracharya*

Contents

Introduction and Intention

I didn't want to write this book.

There—I said it.

In fact, I took a lot of time rejecting the notion and fighting it.

I'll tell you why: although I like writing and teaching leadership and related topics, I didn't like talking about *female leadership.* The topic seemed obtuse: hard to grasp, with few leaders to look up to in today's world. I didn't like the books that were out there on women's leadership, and I would never buy them, because the advice seemed old and canned. Worse, a book on women's leadership seemed like a 1970s battle cry to burn our bras. As much as I tried, I could not shake that vision. We blamed men for not getting ahead; never once did we consider how we contributed to the problem.

Is this as far as we've gotten in 2017?

Since we have no idea how to move forward, we just try to warm up the post-hippie movement? We are women, hear us roar - now give us the leadership position.

No, I didn't want to be any part of it.

Furthermore, when I looked deeply at women's groups—of any kind, be it a seminar, lunch, or meeting—it seemed that they were more about complaining and consoling, not really *doing* anything. Often a group of women gathered who just wanted to bitch, be consoled, and feel better about their lives. My view was that this kind of gathering of women wasn't empowering, but an excuse to not stand up, move forward, and try a different approach. There is an endless supply of self-help books, shows, webinars, and seminars out there that turn out to be a masquerade of "helping" women with problems.

Or worse, the fact that main stream media available today *made women believe they had problems.* Most women didn't have anything wrong with them until they started reading that crap. I found a lot of the women's leadership movement to be a total travesty. To me, women's groups, books, and gatherings reeked of weakness, rather than power.

I feared that if I wrote this book, I'd be designated as the "women's leadership expert," which scared the pants off me. I'm for everyone, not just women— and I mean that. I live that statement.

I've spoken at women's groups, church groups, large conferences, and small settings. I've given talks in synagogues, at large churches of every denomination, and at Hindu business conferences, in any setting you can imagine. From formal seating in ballrooms with crystal chandeliers in country clubs to worn-out, dank basements in churches where AA meetings are also held. I've had the honor and privilege of speaking to people in industries including banking and finance, oil and gas, manufacturing, and engineering, for audiences as small as ten and as large as five hundred. Every age, every shape, every color; trust me when I say, I'm for everyone.

My issue is seeing the division between women and work.

I have boldly stated publicly on radio and in interviews that I would never be the woman with the "Go Girl Power" battle cry. Bottom line: men paid my bills for many, many years. I was invited (and earned) my way into the boys' club. It seemed horribly ungrateful to slap the hand that fed me for so many years by writing a book saying men were awful. Besides, I didn't believe men were the reason we didn't get ahead; *we* were the reason we weren't promoted.

So let's digress for a moment and talk about my exclusive invitation into the boys' club. I know what you're thinking—you saw my photo on the back cover, so let's get this out there right now: I didn't get there because I was pretty or manipulative. I got there *because I knew how to play the game*. I am in on the private jokes among executives; however, I am not THE joke.

Had I gotten there on my looks or my wit, I would be a one-hit wonder and not able to sustain a livelihood. I learned and quickly. So can you.

So, for me to wake up one morning and write a book and put men down didn't make any sense at all.

Ironically, and I admit embarrassingly, I have been told numerous times I am wired much more like a man than a woman. That tendency, along with my drive, got me my success and seat at the table. That exact approach got me clients, book sales, speaking gigs, and money. For many years, all the clients were men.

Something, somewhere along the line changed. My phone started ringing, and now women were on the other end.

In 2013, *seventy percent of my clients were women*, not men, which broke a fourteen-year streak. It used to be that I coached men, and I knew my demographic inside and out: powerful men; men who wanted to make more money; men who had brilliant minds; men who were in upper management making the hard calls who wanted a coach, a confidante, someone they would share their secrets with in total privacy, without judgment. I was deemed as the woman who could read the tea leaves of the job market and help them get the best deal, someone to partner with them and help them hire or build a new team, or help them craft the language to fire the old team because they couldn't stomach it.

They say behind every great man is a great woman. *I* was that woman.

Therefore, the women's leadership movement was not something I wanted to do, ever.

But now women were calling me, asking for career coaching and leadership programs. In 2014, "Leadership Lessons from the Lioness," my own radio show through Plaid for Women, launched with monumental success. I wrote a series of articles that generated the highest traffic on the site.

Women asked me how to navigate their careers, and looked utterly shocked when I told them they were underpaid. They asked about how to deal with a difficult (female) boss. They called when they were about to take their first leadership job and weren't quite sure they could pull it off. My business model changed, and before I knew it, I was launching leadership programs and classes in the Middle East as well as the United States.

And I think leadership is kind of like that: one is elected, and people follow. Deep responsibility seats itself if you have a conscience.

This is where it gets very heavy for me.

It's the *responsibility* that weighs heavily on me, even now as I write the introduction of this book, for once you know better, you are expected to do better.

My great teacher, Shankarachaya, taught me about attitude and intention. He'd hammer me and say, "Why are you doing that? Why are you saying that? Why are you really saying it? Behind every word and deed is your intention. Is it pure? You can never improve on your faulty personality. But you can always work on your intention."

"It's never what people say," he'd tell me. "In fact, just forget that their mouths are moving and stop listening. Look for their intention. Why are they speaking? What is behind the words?"

Being popular. Craving success. Craving money. Being liked. (A biggie for a lot of women.) Fame—fame is a big one. (Just look at Facebook.) Playing the savior. Playing the martyr. Having all the answers. Being the smart girl. Being the do-er. (Which is total crap, and an entire chapter if I get into that topic.) Blindly lying to myself and saying I am helping someone, or that I'm here to impart some great wisdom.

Oh, for God's sake. Really, Elizabeth?

So why write this?

I looked at myself deeply, and it took weeks to answer that question and to be completely honest.

Here is how I see it: there is no one to save. There is no woman who is broken. It's all just moving as it is. Nothing is wrong, therefore, there is no one to help. That's just more ego trip, a little lie that makes one feel bigger than the weaker person, wearing a superwoman cape and thinking you are "helping" them.

Consider this: if you are helping, immediately there is a victim, and you are the savior, and that is the farthest thing from unity.

Let's go even deeper.

There isn't anyone out there. Nope. There isn't. Quantum physics proved that. It's all molecules in motion, squelched up in a conglomerate with a brain that causes the separation that says you are there, and I am standing over here, and we are separate units. It's an illusion, and it's set up that way...but it's not the truth. Don't believe a word I write. Instead, read about Spanda theory or chat with a physicist.

So, why write? Why write this?

These are my intentions:

> I'd like there to be unity in the workforce.
>
> I'd like to live in a place called the "office," where there is less division.

I'd like women to not feel limited by men at work, and pursue a leadership path, if they want one.

I'd like women to see how they get in their own way through their thoughts.

My intention is that this book is an offering to all my sisters, from whom I vainly thought I was separated—which was my mistake.

The intention is to have this book be a guidebook, where your eyes glide along the pages and reveal sound advice, comfort, and courage.

The intention is to help you balance the bitch and the boss, and that the two shall never, ever meet in the office with your team.

The intention is for this book to be uplifting, and that we find as woman a different and successful path to the top while supporting each other, rather than yanking each other back down the ladder.

The intention is to change how we as women show up *in relationship* to leadership in the offices across America, for this is all a part of the play of life.

Most of all, I'd like this book to be thought provoking.

Look, I'm not saying this is THE way into leadership or the RIGHT way or the ONLY way. What I *am* saying is that I have something to offer, and many have benefited.

I am willing to be vulnerable, and share what I learned over the years as a leader (of a team of all men) and as a coach to the most powerful men in America. I'm not someone spouting off or someone who interviewed a bunch of leaders and now is throwing up the information.

I am the female leader.

I've also built teams in companies such as Fiserv, Mentor Graphics, and Intel. Mostly high tech, with sexy sleek company names you'd certainly recognize—I've been behind it, hiring their talent. Usually engineering, but sometimes C-suite. The stock went up or down with my recommendation.

Which can be heavy, *very heavy*, knowing that what you say about someone can get them the job or kill the deal, all because you have that much influential power with executives. As a female leader, I've experienced that everything touches everything, and everything matters.

This book, however, is different.

My joy is in the doing. I'm writing this book for the sheer joy of writing and giving the knowledge away—no strings, no hidden agendas. My intentions are clear.

Whatever comes of this book, be as it may.

Chapter 1

Why Do You Want to Lead?

Every woman looks forward to the day that she gets the promotion, wears the new suit, and takes on a leadership position. Throughout her career, she was told that when she finally makes this quantum leap, she will have "arrived." Oddly enough, corporate America rarely supports nor trains their leaders, but instead promotes people due to political situations.

Before the ink is even dry on the offer letter, amazingly enough, women don't stop and ask themselves *why* they want to lead. It's worth considering your personal motivation as a woman in a leadership role.

People go into leadership for a variety of reasons—they

Think they can do it better than their last boss

Want power over others

Crave the spotlight for accomplishments

Want to make more money

Were accidentally put into the role, and decided to stay

It's shocking that few women think about the drivers leading to the promotion. Instead, most think about what they have to gain as a leader or the money they will make once they get promoted. Few consider what they should give and the challenges that lie ahead, or the responsibility. They get caught up in the glory of the promotion, without thinking ahead about what it *really* entails.

In 2014, I conducted a webinar in the Middle East called, "Moving From Individual Contributor to Leader." The entire point of the presentation was not to explain how to get the promotion, but to slow down everyone in the audience and get them to consider whether they *wanted* the leadership job. There is nothing shameful about being a solid individual contributor.

In July of 2013, The Washington Post published and an article about my favorite female leader, Indra Nooyi, the CEO of PepsiCo. The headline read, "Why PepsiCo CEO Indra K. Nooyi Can't Have It All," and Indra told the truth. The entire article was about her daughter's reaction to her receiving the title of president for the company. Indra was working late, as she had on many nights, and was told her promotion would be announced the next day. Excited, she left the office early with the intention of telling her family. When Indra walked in the door, her family exclaimed, "We are out of milk. Go back out and get some." The story brought up the harsh reality many women face once they get the promotion: Guilt.

Women start to question themselves, wondering if they should participate in family events rather than spending more time at the office. They gradually notice that they are caught up in their work email on their phone rather than watching their kids' soccer games. Work has a way of sucking you in, making you feel needed as a woman. Being needed is a dangerous and seductive trap for every woman.

Work and leadership can give a woman a rush not found at home or in the bedroom, or by being someone's Mommy. Work and perceived power can be an intoxication found nowhere else on earth. It can be a drug, and each day at the office, another fix is administered.

That's about when the guilt starts to set in for women, and they question whether they can really have it all. As women, we keep trying, but Indra is very clear: we can*not*. To keep chasing the notion we can have it all is pure folly. Something has to give. For many women, what gives is them. They give into exhaustion and feeling "less than," which is ironic, because the leadership position was supposed to fulfill them. We believe the little lies saying that if we take the job, we'd be...whatever; fill in the blank. In the end, women feel duped when they get into a powerful role and find there is no support—it can be isolating, and no one will train them. And yet, they blindly chase the leadership role.

"Chasing." Isn't that the key word it all comes down to? Chasing what is outside. Chasing a feeling. Chasing power. Chasing the promotion, then running to keep up with it to prove you are doing a good job. It can become an endless cycle of stress, disappointment, and shame for a woman who naively believes that she can have it all. Buying into the notion that this is our "time" as women and we can have the perfect marriage, the children, the immaculate house, and perfect Thanksgiving and Christmas holidays with our families, as well as be thin and have time to work out, have girlfriends, and be well rounded overall and high functioning.

It's our fault, because we bought into the lie: we read all the magazines and books, and saw all the TV shows. Today, women are coming out in droves in high level leadership positions, which makes us believe: "Well, if she can do it, I can too, right? And if I can't pull off this leadership thing, then there is something very deficient with me as a woman."

3

Men do it—men hold big positions and have families. They appear to have this crazy notion of work/life balance worked out.

Which raises the question, do men feel guilty? This is a tough question to answer, and I think it's worth looking deeper at the issues rather than the question.

Men's roles in American society are set up differently, and their psychological wiring is different. Men are expected to go out, work, and make the most money possible for their family. It's more expected today in the middle class than ever before. The list of demands is high for a man, including not only providing, but also providing comfort and luxury for his family. Years ago, in the 1960s, that was a man's job, to provide. Today men are expected to participate in their marriages as friends as well as lovers, be the "hands-on" Dad, and be effective in the office. Women are taught to support those efforts and set up home life so that even if she has a job, she must figure out how to maintain a proper home, ensure the children are doing their homework, and still be highly engaged at every level. Like it or not, as much as we want to look the other way, there are still pink and blue chores. And women, being women, take it on, along with the guilt.

Indra, hats off to you, as you should be our shining example. Thanks for the reality check about the folly that we really can't have it all, but must instead choose and choose wisely.

Years ago, I went to a gynecologist whom I thought was very successful. She had her own practice, was an accomplished surgeon, spent a lot of time with her patients, and was beautiful. She was my own model, and I decided then and there she was who I wanted to emulate at fifty. I once asked her about her life; she said to me carefully, "Well, Elizabeth, you can't have it all, but you can pick and choose. There is a lot to choose from in life." To my surprise, even my doctor, who I thought had it all, didn't. It was some of the best advice I ever got, at the age of thirty-five.

From my own experience, men look at their careers and job changes very differently than women. In fact, some men I encountered who made job changes made these decisions because of family conversations, rather than from internal guilt: "You missed Billy's game. Do you have to work again tonight?" his wife may ask. A man may take another job, but never with a downgrade in title or a lateral move. He takes a job with a manageable workload, but not a lower position.

Men believe they deserve the paycheck without the guilt and often sleep just fine at night. Women, on the other hand, are a different story.

So how do we get out of the guilt trap? Do we even want to be leaders? That is the mighty question.

What are we doing? Why are we doing it...Why are we *really* doing it?

Leadership isn't about you, and for many, the shock of that notion hits around the ninety-day mark. It's about your deliverables, reporting, and organizing. Performance is measured very differently. Retaining talent on your team is critical, and turnover will quickly become highlighted as a strike against you. Everyone knows a team that turns over eventually points at the leader as the cause, not the team.

The most difficult leap into leadership is letting go of getting external praise or credit, and being able to delegate. Some of the best female leaders are really teachers in disguise. They enjoy getting the team to the goal and working with people individually.

They enjoy growth and welcome it. They see the value in the team and don't take credit for their actions.

Still questioning whether you want to make the leap into leadership, and are floundering to get there? There are many women who long to be a leader in a company, but are constantly passed over.

In June of 2014, *Forbes Magazine* wrote an article called, "Taking Initiative In the Workplace Will Help You." In the article, they reported exactly what I have been stating in many of my speeches over the past year: "Often, these leadership sentiments are not based on our skill levels, but rather social constructs that our superiors hold, which makes them that much more difficult to overcome."

If you read very carefully in between the lines, it's not about our education, nor the lack of training: it's about "social constructs." This means, as women, if we change how we present ourselves, we may be able to break down the social barriers to become promoted. It's not about changing yourself, nor your values; it's about watching your impact and how you are received.

Many times, in TV and radio interviews (as well as private conversations) I've been asked, "Did you have to become more like a man in order to be taken seriously or to lead?"

No. Never. I'd never compromise myself in that way. However, I'm smart enough to sit back and see how others did it, and what worked.

I'll tell you a little secret: fair warning, this comment will likely make you recoil and get angry, but it's the cold hard truth.

Men laugh at us. They find us foolish.

I've tested this above statement by saying it publicly in a room of men and women during one of my talks. Men smile whenever I say this. They know I've got the secret, and I'm telling on them.

Men know that ultimately the beautiful traits that make us women will backfire on us in the office: that passion will be displayed and perceived as anger. One moment of tears in an office will expose us as weak, and that display may never be recoverable. One moment of giving into a hormonal flux will make the men in the office shake their heads and say, "Yeah, this is why we can't promote her. She's inconsistent. Her moods drive her. We need logic."

What some men at the top fail to see is that the thriving companies have both the heart and head at work.

Regardless, this is what keeps holding us back: perception, instability of emotions, and lack of consistency.

Women working in the office is akin to a woman visiting Home Depot looking for a wrench. When she walks into Home Depot, every male in the store knows she is out of place, doesn't know what she is looking for, and may not know how to use the tool. If she asks for help, they will assist. But they know she doesn't know what she is doing. She is out of her element.

Work is like this scenario for most women. While we've come a long way, baby, but we have a lot longer to go.

Men know that a woman can't navigate the system called the office without having emotional outbursts or giving into pure spite. They know a woman will be passed over for promotions because she will indulge in her emotions. This leads men to distrust her immediately. On a football team, this type of player would be banished for a bad attitude.

Men also know a woman cannot negotiate her salary, and if she is offered the leadership job, she will take it for much less than her male counterparts. She's cheap, and she will work like a dog because she has something to prove. They know it, and take advantage of it during negotiations. Still, we take the job, thinking in vain we will "earn our way," which rarely happens.

The earning scenario is very different for a man: he will ask for more money, thinking he deserves it—he's the breadwinner. A woman can be a single mother and struggling, yet she will not be aware of what a position pays and will ask for a lateral move. Then women dare to complain that they are underpaid.

Whose fault is it, really?

Men are always promoted for jobs *above their skill set*. This is an unspoken rule among men. The thought pattern is that a man will have so much pressure to keep his job and provide for his family that he will rise to the occasion. They also believe he will grow into the role. Forty years ago, men were "groomed" into positions by powerful predecessors. Women, on the other hand, view the office as a place to work and constantly prove their skill sets, then ask gracefully for the upper management position. When they are turned down, they just go to their desk and live with it, disgruntled and bitter.

A man's response would be to find another job for more money, quit, and move on. He wouldn't put his trust and faith in the company; he'd drive his own career. Women, on the other hand, will sit at their desks waiting endlessly to be recognized, thinking that if they just worked harder, they will be rewarded.

The result is bitter women.

Women would go a long way by just watching how men operate, rather than arguing and stating how the system is set up unfairly.

Just watch a man. Watch him when he's upset. Watch him as he delivers bad news. Watch him when he has a win for the team.

Can you, as a woman, mimic some of those traits without altering your femininity?

The other big fear women have is being greedy, or, heaven forbid, getting more than they have "earned."

Do you think you don't deserve the promotion, or can't get it?

Do you think you have to become manly to be successful in business? Cold? Ruthless?

Like it or not, a woman cannot get angry at work. She is not deemed passionate, but labeled a "bitch," and later in this book, I'll point to some research on that statement. Men, on the other hand, are viewed very differently if they get upset in the office. Men who get mad are called "passionate." Rather than argue the point about why, women should notice how their delivery on bad news has an impact. Time should be taken to formulate what they are saying and, most importantly, why they are saying it, prior to entering a business meeting of any kind.

This is not manipulation. In fact, it's about caring enough about the other person to slow down and consider what you are about to say and how it will land on the other party. Even after endless books on communication for women that flooded the bookstores in the 1980s and 1990s, and we still can't handle ourselves in a meeting. These books failed us because they taught us that more talking is good; they didn't teach us when to speak, or how silence can be more effective in business.

Consistency is key for others to change their perception of you.

If you are constantly passed up for the promotion, the common denominator is YOU. Take some time and think about how people view you in the office and what their opinions would be. Some of what you view may be hurtful and hard to swallow, but worth it in the long run if you want the promotion.

Look at other women in the company who are successful. Watch how they behave in meetings. Listen to their words. See if they are consistent in their actions. My sense is they are, or else they wouldn't be able to continue in be in power.

A few years ago, I started working with a female client who wanted to move into her position and sync up with her female boss. Christina was not confident in her new promotion, and knew that every move she made in the first ninety days could make or break her. She was a very unusual client and had the inward habit of thinking her life through in its entirety. She witnessed her boss, who sat two short clicks from the CEO of the division. Christina came to me one day and announced she only wanted one more job change in her career path. She wondered out loud how a woman could have a marriage and children and still work sixty hours a week. Her own boss looked exhausted, and was demanding. Christina looked at the salary and the title and decided right then and there that it wasn't worth it. "I can do a good job at one thing, but not many things. I'm concerned when I do have kids. I won't be able to juggle it all."

I came across in the Washington Examiner in December of 2013 that captured Christina's feelings in data, and frankly, it surprised me. It read that fewer young women than young men aspire to become a boss or top manager; "some 34 percent say they're not interested, compared to 24 percent of young men." And the clear majority of adults of all ages who reduced their work hours to care for family members—94 percent—say they are glad they did it.

Thoroughly consider whether you want to be in leadership before you make the jump. It's extremely likely that if you jump into leadership, there will be no development, and you'll have to learn by the school of hard knocks or require a coach to be successful. Remember, it's perfectly fine to be a solid individual contributor.

Sometimes getting the title and pay bump isn't worth it. Christina has a good point: it's difficult to have it all and do it all well.

Chapter 2

How Men Get Ahead (At Work)

I distinctly remember coming home from the office one day and talking about work with my husband. At the time, I lead a team of seven—consisting mainly of men—and I had concerns about my leadership. I don't remember what the story was about, but I do remember being very concerned that the team would sense that I favored the highest performer. How could I not favor Chris? He was excellent at his job, respected me, didn't push back, and when we were in a pinch, he delivered, quickly and accurately. My concern was that others would notice and there would be competition.

My husband explained to me in a very simple manner that there could only be one Peyton Manning, and that all men know this.

I looked at him blankly.

"You know who Peyton Manning, is, right, Elizabeth?"

"Yeah, he's the quarterback."

"He is one of the *best* quarterbacks. Everyone knows it. The point is, all the other football players know it, too. There is no strife on the team, because they all KNOW there can only be one Peyton Manning, and that their jobs are equally important. They know their value; therefore, there is no internal competition. This is the core reason why women don't work well with other women— there is too much competition. Men know how to be on a team and get along. Don't worry about your team. All the guys know there is only one Chris. If you make the others know their value and make them feel equally important, you'll never have an issue. The other guys will settle down and get to work."

My husband also taught me that the most important player on the team was not the quarterback: it was the left tackle. The left tackle is responsible for watching the quarterback's blind spot. This made total sense to me when I thought about politics in the office and how football related to work.

I gave this concept some thought and my husband was right. At that exact moment, I planned a new approach with the team, and I even identified my left tackle.

My husband continued, "Men can fight and get very physical on the football field, but at the end of the game, they can go drink beer together and put it aside. Two lawyers can fight in courtroom, and go have a drink afterwards and laugh about it. Women cannot, for whatever reason. As little boys, we are taught teamwork and sportsmanship. We view the office the same way: we don't care who is prettier or smarter, or who has more friends at work. We just buckle down and do what needs to be done."

Two men with big egos can dislike each other and work side by side and accomplish goals, but two women never can. If they don't like or trust each other—if one emotion is out of place—this makes or breaks the project they are working on together.

I got to thinking about that deeply. While little boys are out learning how to work on cars and play sports, young women aren't viewed or encouraged to engage in that way. In America, little girls are encouraged to be princesses and are not necessarily rewarded for being smart. In some odd way, little girls are programmed to think attracting a mate is the most important skill she can attain.

Nothing comes from nothing.

Here are some sobering statistics from the news media that illustrate as girls grow into women, they are influenced by what they are exposed to.

Teenagers spend

  Thirty-one hours a week watching TV

  Seventeen hours a week listening to music

  Three hours a week watching movies

  Ten hours a week online

In total, a teenager spends ten hours and forty-five minutes on media consumption every day.

The bigger concern is the *quality* of the images of women portrayed through the media in America. Media is paid for by advertisers, and the aim of advertising is to make the viewer feel small and suggested that buying their product solves the "problem." Think about all the commercials you've seen where a woman is the hot object. Girls get the impression at a young age that it's important to be pretty and how they look is important to their success and survival. Their worth is tied to how they look, which is a trap, because age will set in, leaving them feeling robbed. In return, boys get the notion that beauty is important for a young woman as well. Americans in general value looks over intellect. Once you are old, you are washed up, according to our society. This mad cycle keeps perpetuating as the media creates and churns out unrealistic expectations, and we continue to unconsciously consume these illusions.

So what happens to a little girl's attitudes after continuous exposure to notions implanted by the media?

Seventy-four percent of girls say they are under pressure to please everyone (Girls Inc, The Supergirl Dilemma)

Ninety-eight percent of girls feel there is an immense pressure from external sources to look a certain way (National Report on Self Esteem)

Ninety-two percent of teen girls would like to change something about the way they look, with body weight ranking the highest. (Dove campaign, Heart of Leadership.Org)

I know what you are thinking: what does this have to do with adult women, work, and leadership positions?

Everything.

Here are the results of these influences on women in the United States:

Only thirty-seven of women have ever served as *state* governors (Center for American Women and Politics, Wikipedia)

While sixty-seven countries around the world have had women as presidents or prime ministers. China, Afghanistan, and Iraq have more women in government than the United States.

Part of the issue is it's difficult for an American to envision a woman in politics, without focusing on what she looks like claimed the documentary "Miss Representation." In the film, according to Condoleezza Rice, "The candidate running and the country would have to have a psychological breakthrough." In politics women are called "bitchy;" the idea is that leadership is for men.

Ironically, at seven years old, both little boys and little girls want to be president of the United States. By fifteen, however, there is a huge divide.

What we think about, as women, we bring about. You can only create as much as you can envision, and I think it starts with us.

Of all the research and study that I put into this book, the statistics that sadden me the most are:

Only fourteen percent of CEO executives are women (CNN Money, March 24, 2014)

Three percent of positions with clout in the mainstream media—telecommunications, entertainment, publishing, and advertising—are held by women

Three percent of creative directors within ad agencies are women (Advertising Age)

Twenty-nine percent of American firms are owned by women, yet they employ only 6% of the country's workforce and account for barely 4% of business revenues (this is roughly the same share they contributed in 1997). (The Economist/2013 State of Women Owned Businesses)

Eighty percent of all purchasing decisions are made by women (Forbes).

Isn't it ironic that according to these statistics, women have power in purchasing decisions, but little power when it comes to high level positions in corporate America and legislature?

If we women raised little girls who were taught to value being smart over pretty, would our self-esteem issues vanish? Regardless, the time to act is *now* as we women look at how we view ourselves and help each other into leadership positions at work. By grooming, training, and promoting each other, we can take our talents into the workplace and thrive, not just barely survive.

During my own career, I observed men carefully, and credit this approach to my success. Frankly, I didn't have a choice. It was mostly men in my industry and men that I sold to, because there weren't a lot of women in power in corporate America at the Director of Vice President level. To succeed, I had to figure out how to sell to men and how they bought a service, which is vastly different from women's buying behaviors.

Furthermore, I watched how men gained confidence and respect at work, and I think there is a lot for women to gain from careful consideration of how men navigate an office, without sacrificing our identities. Most days, I just wished we dropped all the gender differences and focused on developing better leaders; however, the divide and issues that women face cannot be ignored.

Instead of taking it in and applying a different approach, we somehow seem to form groups that do nothing but complain about the problem. There is this huge line that divides men and women. Women react by getting upset about unfair pay and treatment, and get stuck in our feelings, even with our ability to move forward and make some real change. I'm suggesting it's our reactions to what has occurred that keeps us stuck—in the office, the media, and worse—in ourselves.

Our solution for many years has been to form groups of consolation, not true groups of empowerment. We look for escape from the pain and the feel-good fix, but nothing gets accomplished. We talk and gather, thinking this will make us feel better. The result? Nothing has really changed.

My sincere desire is to bring about change by forming a new approach and new ideas when it comes to work.

In 2015 I wrote an article entitled, "Women, Work and Guilt" https://www.linkedin.com/pulse/20140730131027-2821170-women-work-and-guilt) which was read by thousands on LinkedIn, Plaid for Women, and CERM, a quality magazine. I openly commented that women bought into a bad rap: we owned feeling guilty at work. Find a woman who never feels guilty about something and you will find a man, and sadly, it's true.

We get in our own way. We—not men—keep us from holding powerful positions. It's time to stop blaming the ex-husband that put you down, the boss who didn't promote you, or the guilt that racks your heart whenever you drop your young child off to daycare as you head for work. We need to own this. It's time to stop the madness.

Rather than being hostile to men who are in leadership positions, my suggestion is we learn from them. Watch them. See what they do. Invite one to lunch. Ask him a business question. Pick his brain. You'll be surprised. He'll let you.

Rather than gathering and forming yet another networking group (which is really a bitch session), I suggest that we start seriously considering other women in the organization to promote. Groom the younger, beautiful women up into the next role. You know which women I'm talking about—the younger, talented women who could quickly climb the ladder. Park your feelings of inadequacy for the good of the whole. Witness your feelings, but don't act on them. Identify top performing women outside of Human Resources, and promote women in IT, Accounting, and Engineering.

This is a tall order, and I've certainly had my own battle with the green-eyed monster. Recently in my own office, we hired a junior recruiter. She is young, single, and beautiful, lives in Uptown Dallas, drives a white Mercedes, and has her whole life in front of her at the ripe age of 28. She has the good fortune of having affluent parents, a college education, and the support of her family and boyfriend for her career endeavors.

And for the first time, I must admit I felt middle aged sitting next to her. Stinking thinking consumed me.

Instead of believing these thoughts and feelings, I quit looking at her and looked at myself. I turned within and asked myself the hard questions: Why am I jealous? What is this feeling about? She is just a mirror by which I could look deeper inside myself. I realized the divide was only caused in my mind, and wasn't real at all.

Furthermore, I started to listen and watch her with my heart, embracing her, instead of shrinking away and being hateful. By 5 p.m., I saw her and her view of herself through her conversations with me. Her own insecurities were bleeding all over everything on the first day of the job: her constant worry about whether she'll marry the boyfriend, knowing her time was ticking. The nagging feeling of wondering whether she was doing things right in her life. Questioning her first day on the job, feeling like she didn't know anything.

Didn't I feel that way at 28?

Instead of judging her and rejecting her, couldn't I embrace her—and, dare I suggest—teach her something so she is empowered on the job? What is the best for everyone in this situation?

19

In that moment, I decided not to listen to the vain thoughts in my head that were clearly my ego. I didn't want to be small and narrow. I wanted to expand and live what I believe. That very day, I reached out to her, taught her a few tricks, and got to know her as a person.

All women have value.

All women can be phenomenal leaders.

It starts with working together and putting aside petty notions about each other and ourselves.

Chapter 3

Why Women Compete

Research has shown us the deep psychological roots of competitiveness between women. Noam Shpancer, in his *Psychology Today* article entitled, "Feminine Foes: New Science Explores Female Competition", pointed out the main reason why women compete and disparage each other: to attract a mate. When a woman moves into full competition stance, she executes two primary displays: self-promotion and competitor degradation.

How does this play out in the office?

Let's say a new admin is hired. She is extremely attractive, youthful, charming, and dresses well. Men in the office notice her cheerfulness, and perhaps even find her attractive. Tenured women will subconsciously alienate her and make a point of stepping over her if the situation presents itself. Others sneer and say that the admin likely got hired because she was sleeping with the boss. If there is a small group of women who are "in," they will give her the cold shoulder. Over time, the younger woman, often confused, will fade into the woodwork at the office, and tend to eat lunch alone.

I've personally been that twenty-something woman in my first office job, and distinctly remember the company having a "woman's luncheon" and not getting invited. They stuck me to answer the phones during the lunch hour and never even brought me back a plate of food. Think back: Have you experienced this from another woman in the office?

Competition with other women plays out in a variety of ways. They can be so subtle that, unless you were looking to find it, they would go unnoticed. Self-promotion is another way women compete. Something as benign as a networking meeting can reveal a competitive setting. For example, a small group of people are standing around talking about business-related issues, and a woman joins them. Trying to be a part of a conversation, she may try to interject something witty. Another woman, seeing this and feeling her own insecurities, may speak louder or draw attention to herself. It may be socially acceptable, but it sets the stage for one-upmanship between two women.

I, myself, became prey to this behavior early in my career. Preferring to be around men, I alienated women and had "guy friends." The alienation was likely on both sides: women didn't like me, and I didn't like working with them, at all. Often, I was the one in the office who was alienated from women, and I found them to be jealous and overly emotional. Many times, I didn't understand it, and although I never intended to upset them or make them jealous, somehow, I did. Subconsciously, these office situations reminded me of my mother, whom I didn't like on some level. Her wild emotions and unpredictable behavior made an unstable household, which was only more exacerbated when she drank. The odd fact was I turned out to be nothing like her, so I never understood her, and to make things worse, I had no empathy for my mother. Many years later I discovered that her emotional behavior was due to her big and sensitive heart: when situations arose, she felt, deeply. To survive mentally and emotionally, I had to reject her. The best way to reject someone permanently is to dislike them. As a child and even into my adulthood, I found her foolish and judged her life as a train wreck. I could never rationally understand why she couldn't see how she created such turmoil. Fast forward to my working life: when I encountered an emotional woman at work, it was a huge turn-off.

Because I didn't embrace women in the office or have empathy, or join their groups in any way, I was immediately an outcast. This set up an ongoing pattern for years, and to some level hindered my career.

I never understood the competitive game that was played, and once or twice, due to my lack of knowledge of how women were wired with this competitiveness, I got fired. This only made my desire to work for men stronger, and added to my own confusion. I didn't enjoy working with women and preferred working with men, finding them less emotional and more rational. I never found myself lost or confused when I worked with or for a man. I can't say the same for working with women; however, I have had some excellent female bosses during the last ten years in my career.

My Myers-Briggs type didn't help, either. If you aren't familiar with Meyers Briggs, basically it's a test that spits out four letters and is based off Carl Jung's formula. It measures strengths and limitations based off your behavior, which in turn makes the test results scary accurate. It turns out my type was rare, only making up one to three percent of the overall population; and of this one to three percent, most were men, not women. Low emotion, highly rational approach, and strong follow-through made me act more like a man than a woman, even though my physical form was very feminine. I was as confused as my audience when I opened my mouth and spoke or closed a business deal. With these contradictory tendencies, right out of the gate I was misunderstood, and I felt alone. However, looking back now, I know I also perpetuated the pattern.

In the same article *Psychology Today* article entitled, "Feminine Foes: New Science Explores Female Competition", Joyce Benenson, a researcher at Emmanuel College in Boston chimed in.

Her study around this phenomenon concluded that women in competition showed three unique characteristics. Women would move into aggression that wasn't physical to protect their bodies or purposely not promoting other women who were attractive; and finally, resorting to socially alienating other women and excluding them completely.

Check, on all three. Yes, I've been on the receiving end of all that.

Looking at life today in the United States, I see that although our internal hard wiring makes women compete with one another, that wiring is no longer needed in this paradigm. As women, we don't *need* to compete for a man. There are plenty out there, and there is plenty of access to men through dating sites and other social functions. No one should ever worry whether they will get married. Furthermore, we have proven we can earn our own living and even raise children without a mate. We can even choose through science to go to a clinic and have sperm inseminated into us without having the traditional family setting. We aren't June Cleaver, and don't have to be. Shortly stated, we don't need men for money, children, or survival any more.

This is my strong statement: we don't need men for *anything anymore*.

Although it's in our biology to compete, does it need to be our ideology?

There is a grave consequence to continue being asleep at the switch. Giving into our competitive, catty natures will stagnate us as women, and this continues the destructive behavior of not identifying and promoting each other into positions of power.

In the end, it's a house of mirrors.

We talk a great deal about women who are similar to the descriptions above, but what are we *personally* doing, day by day, moment by moment, so that the infection doesn't spread?

Muktananda was a great Indian saint and an avatar who came to the United States. He wrote many books, which I have read. For me, his books keep my mind in the right disposition to move through the world.

The passage quoted below gave me a very distinct vision of why I act the way I do and how everything touches everything. While many times I have experienced this, Muktananda drove the point home, and to this day, reading this makes me pause about my own behavior with women. I no longer want to be a part of the problem, and frankly, I had a big mess that I created of my own in the world that I needed to clean up.

Here is a direct excerpt from his book:

> I am reminded of a verse from Krishnasuta, who says, "In the world one becomes one's own enemy and begins to treat everyone else with hostility." Because of your own perversity you begin to look upon everyone else perversely; you project your own faults onto other people. As a result, you begin to see faults even in those who have none, you begin to see impurities even in those who are pure. Whatever man does for or against another, he really does for or against himself....

I am reminded of a story of a palace of mirrors as told by Swami Rama Tirtha: a large, violent, and brutal dog got into the palace of mirrors. He shouldn't have been allowed to go in, but somehow, he did.

He was surrounded by mirrors on all sides. He ran in one direction, and he saw many other dogs running at him. Then he ran in a different direction, and he found just as many dogs running at him. Then he ran a different direction, and he found just as many dogs running at him from that direction.

Then he ran a third direction, and he saw the same thing. He looked upward, and he saw many dogs looking down at him; they frightened him.

He stopped running and wondered what he could do to save himself. He began to bark in sheer terror, and as he barked, he found thousands of dogs barking at him from all sides. This enraged him. It made him mad. He began to jump up and down, and thousands of dogs around him jumped up and down. He kept jumping up and down. Finally, he collapsed.

When the watchman found the corpse, he threw it outside.

This is exactly the condition of everyone in this world.

This last line stopped me dead in my tracks.

This is exactly the condition of the world, and I am a part of this world. *I* do this.

The difference is, I know I do this and no longer want to do this. Over time, I quit doing it. I could slow down my thoughts enough to catch when I was about to engage in this damaging behavior, which ironically would only hurt myself, because "she" is *me*.

We as women need to stop being barking dogs with one another. See your small self as it is, and push it aside to unify yourself with another. Your small self is your ego, but you are much larger than that.

Try this by:

> Noticing when a younger woman comes to you, and you recoil out of jealousy
>
> Coaching another woman, even when you don't think you have time
>
> Identifying key women with talent and promoting them to positions of power
>
> Seeing each woman as your sister, creating unity where there once was division
>
> Stop talking about the problem, and quietly be the solution

Talking never got us anywhere.

Years ago, I quit talking. I stopped kidding myself that I was a great "communicator." Like everyone else, I spent countless dollars on books, tapes, and talks on the topic of communication, finding that these only built more tools and tricks of ways of expressing myself. It built more ego and caused more pain and destruction.

My great teacher said, "Talking never worked anything out. If you pay attention, you'll find talking will often make things worse. Much worse. Have you worked it out, ever? No. People spend countless hours trying to work on their relationships and never really feel satisfied. That would leave one to believe that working it out doesn't happen by working it out *outside*. It would lead one to believe that working it out means working it out *within yourself*."

I will be forever grateful for those words. Months later I found myself about to start a heated argument with my beloved husband, and I stopped myself. Rather than goad him into anger and attack him, I stopped and thought: Wait! Why am I doing this? I can't work this out with him. Why am I so angry? I looked at me and began to work it out within myself, which spared us having a terrible evening.

There is no one out there. It's all a house of mirrors.

We know this on some level. Fast forward to today and we've all experienced quotes about unity, all of which have made some impression on us. I believe all women have picked up a self-help book or two and read the message that the problem is us. But can we take that simple thought and drive it home?

And can we start to live at the office and embrace other women? Can we be watchful enough to know when our biology to compete creeps up, and catch it before it damages another woman, leaving her hurt and confused?

It's not men that prevent us from getting ahead, it's us, and frankly, we can do better than this. We don't need men for money, because we can make our own money. Having a man doesn't mean our survival will be better or worse. Sometimes as women our fear of being without a man is so high, we'll mate with anyone just to save ourselves from being alone. It's shocking to me every time I see this play out. I've seen it with women in their twenties, and in their fifties after their divorce. There is a stench of panic in these women needing to be married by Wednesday. I find the conflict in us amusing: we want men and we blame them. At work, we turn around and blame a man for our lack of financial success.

The data is clear that women don't need men *financially.* The near-equal pay for young women is being driven in large part by their educational gains. Some 38 percent of women ages twenty-five to thirty-two now hold bachelor's degrees, compared to 31 percent of young men. As a result, 49 percent of employed workers with at least a bachelor's degree in 2015 were women, up from 36 percent in 1980. **That means more women in higher-skilled, higher-paying positions.**

The current ratio of hourly earnings for young women to young men, now at 93 percent, is up from 67 percent in 1980, and is the highest in government records dating back to at least 1979.

So, if we don't need men for money, and competition isn't necessary for survival of our species, why not stop the madness?

It's a simple concept, but hard to put into action.

So how do we try to move forward?

Moment to moment.

That's what I've found, personally: it's all moment to moment. Keeping the idea alive in my mind of unity. Slowing down when I'm in a situation at work. Stop speaking. Stop reacting. Respond. Something as small as re-reading an email or instant message before I hit "Send" to check my tone.

Asking myself the hard questions: if I send this out there, does this bring me closer to this person, or am I just screaming my point of view?

There are a lot of days I don't do this well at all. There are some days I am flat out of patience, tired, or just ready for Friday. There are some days where I long to be alone and not around anyone. I trip. I fall. Now I notice it immediately and am very sorry for my small error. Although small, that energy now went out, and I'm responsible for it and what I said or did, or how the look on my face now impacted another person.

I pick myself up, dust myself off after reflecting on my mistake, and try, try again. Never will I fix my quirky personality, but I can always work on my intentions. It's never-ending. No weekends off, no time off for good behavior, no smoke breaks. It's constantly looking at where I'm at with other women, observing how I engage, replaying conversations and the looks on their faces, trying to add something positive when I see another woman struggling, weighing when to keep my mouth shut and when to console.

Moment to moment.

Chapter 4

Playing the Game

> Rule number one as a woman at work: Be aware that there is a game being played in the office.

> Rule number two: Understand the rules.

> Rule number three: Play the game.

It's always been a mystery to me that few women know there is a game that is played at work, and yet they are highly relationship oriented. Men know the game, because they set up the game. From the 1980s, when women entered the workforce in droves, to now, somehow, they missed the memo.

The bottom line is that men rule the world at work, and although we know this, it makes us angry. We secretly think that men have the power and won't give us ours. That anger bleeds all over everything in the office and becomes apparent, which can be a career stall for women. Without knowledge of why she isn't promoted, a woman can't seem to get ahead. If she leaves one company for another, she will find that wherever she goes, she takes that perspective with her. Understanding that there is a game, and that this whole office thing is play, can add a refreshing perspective to everything from office politics to being laid off. It's the mindset that women need to adopt to be successful.

Another broad misconception women have is that there are only so many seats at the table, and men won't let them join. That isn't true at all, and the scarcity mindset hurts us. There are plenty of opportunities for us at work and we should earn them. This doesn't mean working harder, either. It's more about managing our perceptions at work and being credible. Time and consistency is the key. Having the occasional slip-up is okay as well. The pattern, however, needs to be stable. Emotional women don't do well in the office. The workplace is extremely unforgiving if you slip up as a woman, whereas a man can recover. For example, a man can have an outburst and be called "passionate." He can get downright angry and beat his fists on his desk. If a woman does that, well, we all know what happens. She is called a bitch. Again, it's a sad fact, but knowing that is a part of the game a well.

What is the game?

The game is being able to see the team. The team is the company. Not your department or your project, but the overall organization. Men get this concept due to team sports. For women, this is a new thought. We are accustomed to competition and taking each other down through our comments and judgments of each other, which are spawned out of our own insecurities. Two men with big egos can work side by side and create something because they understand the value of the team, but two women cannot, and it's a shame. It's something that as individuals we need to work on.

Make no mistake; there are rules to the game in the office.

Rule number one: While one is on the team, the rules of engagement are getting along and not letting petty differences divide the team. I know that sounds simple, but consider it deeply. This means sending terse emails to each other at work with underlying tones are not acceptable, because that would impede the team. No matter how irritated you are with that jerk at work, don't let that bleed through. Figure out a way to get along and work with them. They can still be a jerk. It's how you manage yourself. In fact, they can be a supreme jerk, and if you handle it well, everyone around you in the office will take note of the jerk, not the situation. You will emerge unscathed.

Rule number two: Never allow internal competition to arise between team members. External market competition is a good thing, but internally it can cause big problems. Never compete. Know your value on the team and that your position is every bit as important as another. No one is higher or lower and everyone has to pull their weight. Men get this. Just look at football and how they celebrate after a touchdown. *They all celebrate.* No one is jealous because one person ran with the ball. The blockers know the quarterback couldn't run with the ball without them blocking. They have their own internal confidence. They know who they are and what they do well, and they don't become scrappy.

Rule number three: The final rule in the game that is there is enough for everyone. Which means there is a seat for you at the table, you can get promoted, and there is enough of everything in the game. While you can do your job well, the only thing stopping you from moving ahead is you. Men know this. They will talk openly about promotions and career growth. They are open about those conversations and don't wait for review time. They perform, watch, network within the company, and go after another role. They watch their political capital and know when they can burn some. The wisest of the tribe know that being highly liked and competent will get them ahead, and they use their relationship skills to leverage a promotion. In their minds, they deserve the promotion and will rise to the occasion, even if it's a little over their heads.

I would be less than honest if I didn't point out that not all companies have cultures that support the above rules to the game. In high performing companies such as Apple, Google, and Microsoft, it's clear there is a game that is played to the highest, and the result is the stock market numbers. People who work for high performing cultures tend to be in high performing companies. Sure, there are plenty of offices we could all point to that have bullies, massive dysfunction, and egos going awry. But even then, if you look subtly, there is a dance going on, a game being played.

My theory of the office being a game is just a way of reframing the situation and pointing out how men approach the office in general, and if you watch closely, this plays out in multiple conversations, meetings at the C level, and even in hiring decisions. It is how men are wired. The office is just another area of place to play, gain accolades and accomplishments, and win at the game called the stock market. If we as women could reframe how we see work, the leadership positions would come easier.

If we knew there was a game, we could get ahead. If we could master our emotions and manage our perceptions, rather than getting caught up in the specifics, we'd progress a lot further. If we worked together and saw each other as a team-mate, we'd promote each other quicker. If we witnessed men and the game, we'd stop the division and the anger in the office. If just once we identified a key woman in a powerful position in the office and took her to lunch and ask, "How did you do it?" we would be ahead.

A dear friend of mine knew I was writing this book and asked me to write on office politics. I realized that would be impossible, because office politics is situational and perceived differently by everyone. That's when my theory of seeing the office as a game came into focus: politics will never be won. But seeing the office as a place where a woman can play the game may be a better framework and take the pressure from the art of mastering politics.

Confidence, real confidence, plays a big part in playing the game. Knowing that there is enough stems from confidence. Not competing with others for petty reasons comes from inner confidence. Believing that you are on a team comes from confidence, as does knowing that your part plays into the bigger whole. It has value; you have value.

Ultimately, it's letting go of our preconceived notions and moving into unity—with each other, with men, with the office. Unity with this thing called life, how we interact in relation to situations and things.

The last conversation I had with Stephen Schettini, the author of *The Naked Monk*, drove this point home. Stephen spent years in a Buddhist monastery and took vows. Years later he disrobed and joined the worldly life. What he found was that wearing the cloak of a tradition was easier than navigating the world. He asked me one day on Skype, "How are you?" What he really meant was, *where are you at with all of it?*

This is what it comes down to, after all.

Where are we at with all of it? What is our perception? What's really going on?

Chapter 5

Why Women Aren't Taken Seriously

Every woman knows the feeling of being overlooked or run over in a meeting. No one likes it, especially executive women.

In 2014, *Harvard Business Review* (HBR) surveyed more than seven thousand people, including female executives at or above the vice president level. The consistent feedback was that women feel less acknowledged during meetings. Although men agreed with this opinion, they disagreed with why women didn't feel powerful.

Apparently, there is this thing called the "meeting before the meeting," and women in executive positions hardly know this goes on. Men do. In fact, men have side-bar conversations prior to a large meeting all the time. Doing this allows them to understand their peers' positions and support on issues that will inevitably be brought up. It's a political way of saving face, while knowing who your internal competitors are in the office.

After reading the article, I looked at past moments of my own career, and I distinctly remembered being invited to one of these private meetings. A manager called me a day before a large staff meeting and asked me directly, "What is your opinion on this issue?" and "Here is what I'm willing to support." This was smart on his part, because I was clearly waving around a lot of hefty data points that could make him look bad. But I've got to say, the conversation with the manager itself, with its brutal candor, surprised me. More than anything, it made me feel included.

When I asked other vice presidents and directors about this male-driven practice during my own research, they agreed this was common, and the fact that I was invited to such a meeting meant I had certainly earned the right.

The men's comments about women in meetings on the HBR survey were enlightening. They said:

Women need to be concise and to the point

Men are afraid of how women will react to criticism

Women need to speak informally and off the cuff.

Women are emotional and defensive when challenged

Women are not as confident as men

Women are too emotional

On the flip side, women's comments about men and office meetings were:

We don't get feedback when we ask for it

We can't get a word in during the meeting

It's not emotion, it's passion

We obsess over a meeting after it's been over for days

We are outnumbered by men at the table; therefore, we tend to not feel "at the table"

These comments are very telling. In fact, everything you need to know about your perception in a meeting, as a woman, is right here in print.

How do we women close the perceived gap?

Watching what we say and how we say it is a good starting point. Men look to executives in leadership to have opinions and deliver them. Being the wallflower in a meeting is not the best plan. Being noticed for the right reasons and having quiet confidence is the best strategy. Remember, the moment you walk in the door to the meeting, men may have expectations of how you may act. It's not you. But you may have to overcome precedents that were set by other women before you came along.

To overcome preconceived notions in meetings with men, consider saying:

"I strongly recommend..."

"I completely agree, and here's why..."

"My plan is..."

"The strategy is..."

Slight changes in communication will project confidence, and over time you'll build political capital.

How a woman physically carries her body makes a difference. Look at old pictures of yourself. Do you slouch? I distinctly remember my husband commenting on how straight my back was on a TV interview. That small act portrayed confidence. Honestly, my host was nearly a foot taller than I was, and I was trying to mirror her with my body. As silly as it sounds, animals do this: they will puff up or become taller to scare away an enemy.

Giving firm, but not bone-breaking, handshakes sends a message in business as well. Having your limbs fold openly projects confidence. Notice how you hold your hands in your lap during a meeting.

What messages are you subliminally sending?

One obvious factor on making or breaking confidence is how a woman dresses. This can be as tricky, as it is a personal choice—it is impossible to control everyone's perception. Years ago, when I worked for an international agency as a headhunter, the owner insisted that we all wear navy blue suits. Not pant suits, but actual skirts or dresses with a matching jacket suit. Two suits were to be expensed each year. Shoes were to be black or navy, and there were no exceptions. New employees always balked that the notion was ridiculous, but the female owner of this successful firm was quite right. She knew that if we all wore business suits, we would be listened to and not stared at. It was her way of controlling the necklines and hemlines of the women who worked for the agency, so we could never be misconceived as inappropriate or vying for business with our bodies. She knew that navy sent the message of a banker or a business man and immediately evoked trust and respect. She knew the reputation of the women who were representing her firm was more important than the latest fashion style. She was right in every way. Dressing in that manner made a solid first impression and allowed me to earn business and keep it. Every man that met me for lunch knew I was there for business, not a date.

I'll never forget the day my biggest client told me that during the recession my competitors wore things that showed a lot of cleavage. Sure, he let them take him to lunch, but he didn't do business with them. He found them to be a joke. Outraged that he shared this with me I asked, "Why on earth would you share with me what my competitor wears and admit you had lunch with her?"

He laughed at my own insecurity and said, "You should know who else is out there and what they do."

He was right. This, too, was a part of the game. Once I got over myself I realized he gave me a very important piece of competitive intelligence, and how that strategy worked on him: it didn't. Smart talk and delivery is what kept him coming back for more.

And all the time I wore the suit I worried that my clients would think I was an idiot for wearing the same thing every time they saw me. No one ever commented, and what I eventually realized was they didn't see the suit at all: they heard me.

Recently, I've found that nobody really sees each other despite the endless videos, selfies, and photos of ourselves on the Internet and stored on our phones. No one really cares. What I've found is that people are wrapped up in themselves. It doesn't take a lot of effort to be invisible. In fact, I find the more digital we become, the less people look and really see anything they remember.

To illustrate this point of being invisible, I played a trick on a woman I went to high school with more than twenty years ago. My theory was that people don't really see who you are, and frankly don't care: they have enough of their own selfish motives going on and playing out in their minds. I predicted my old classmate would never see me, even if I were right under her nose. My best friend and I argued over this. She thought that the friend from high school would know who I was immediately, and I bet twenty bucks she wouldn't. Kind of like wearing the same blue suit repeatedly to every meeting, as I described earlier.

Jenny and I went to high school together, and although we weren't good friends, I would certainly say we were friendly. Her father taught a biology class and was well known throughout the school. Many times, I passed her in the hallways at school or bumped into her at a party. That day, I dared my friend Carolyn to bring me into the store that Jenny now owned as part of a small family business. My theory was that Jenny wouldn't care about who I became as an adult, nor would she recognize me. Boldly I walked into the store and wandered around. It was clear Carolyn and I were together, but Jenny did not pay attention to me. On three separate occasions Jenny stood within three feet of me without realizing that we had been classmates or who I was, even though I contacted her and did engage her.

In fairness, part of this may be because the context: she didn't expect me to drop into her store some twenty years after high school. If I had stood physically in front of our high school, this might have jogged her memory. Ultimately, I was, for all purposes, invisible.

The lesson is to get noticed for the right reasons if you choose to be noticed – especially at work. Being invisible isn't a good option.

What you wear will get you noticed at work. It could even land you the promotion. Personally, I'm not sure exactly when, but the suit became passé years ago. Women now wear dresses or slacks, not suits, for business. For example, I was giving a talk with a CIO who was female, and during our last call before the presentation I shared with her that I would not be wearing a suit. She admitted she still had a small handful of suits in the back of her closet. She couldn't bring herself to get rid of them just yet. I, too, have the same classic suits that take up space in the back of my closet because I can't bear to throw them out.

Be careful with colors, jewelry, and the length of the dress. Watch the height of the heel and the message you are sending. Consider what is the most important: being heard or being admired.

Do the "bend-over check" in the mirror. If you bend over and too much is sticking out in front or in back, don't wear it. If at any time you wonder critically if you are too fat to wear the outfit, don't wear it. I'm guilty of this as well—a handful of dresses in the back of my closet that are just a tiny bit too tight. I don't wear these until I've shed about five pounds. Personally, for me there is nothing worse than a trendy, hip outfit on a woman who is a few pounds too heavy. It screams, "I'm not what I used to be, but I'd like to think I am, so I threw this on and walked out this morning." Portraying confidence is everything, and for a woman what she wears does equate to how she presents.

It's a fine balance to be a woman at work and be successful, but it's worth considering the smallest details. Even something as benign as flirting in the office can quickly derail a woman's credibility, particularly if she holds a managerial position. Carefully weigh the consequences of your actions in the office.

Lastly, not all men will react favorably with a woman in power. Some of them have mommy issues, and you'll certainly know what I speak of if you encounter it. These men will push back, embarrass or discredit you, or flat out ignore you. Know this has NOTHING TO DO WITH YOU. You are merely a catalyst for them to work out their issues, and I strongly suggest you be a gracious teacher for their lessons to bear fruit. Never, ever, take it personally, because that will set up a storm in the office. Do not befriend nor belittle them. Instead just leave them be.

What I found in years of leading men was that if they had healthy ideas of women stemming from their own mothers then typically they were not threatened and would be just fine reporting to a woman. Some men who reported to me had married extremely powerful women whom they openly and publicly admired. When I was in a leadership role years ago, I looked carefully at my team and I saw that each man could report to me easily. When I learned more about their upbringing and whom they married as adults, it all made sense. Some shared with me their upbringing and how their mothers held together the entire household. Two of them, as kids, lived only with their single mother. While the upbringing of the men on my team served me well, these men also knew I was fearless and would protect them to the end, and I did.

Be aware that not all men like women in power. Men tend to compete against each other and may be a little out of sorts competing with you. Connecting with men on that level can instantly level the playing field and can cause a few bruised egos. Just make sure if you are going to compete with a man and get into a heated discussion in a high visibility meeting, it's imperative that you bring your A game. Sometimes it's best to talk in those meetings; other times it's best to stay silent. Weigh the pros and cons of either approach. At all times, measure your perceptions in the office and be extremely aware.

I had my own run-in with a man lacking in confidence who didn't like working with women. I got myself into a pickle at a conference full of PhDs in Washington, DC. As the speaker, I was asked to deliver a talk on leadership. All the other speakers were engineers with PhDs. One speaker flew out from Australia and was going to speak on how to run a board meeting. His presentation was on how he moved from being a corporate leader into academia.

We met and shook hands politely and professionally. Honestly, I didn't think twice about it, thinking this was just another conference. Within a few minutes, I noticed he was talking fast and loud. Looking very closely, I noticed his hands were trembling. His conversation was about his accomplishments and his tenure, and I realized he had something to prove—to me. Finally, after I smiled and listened to him go on and on, he realized that I may be competing as a speaker with him. Naively, I had assumed we were both equals and colleagues. It never occurred me to compete with another speaker. Whatever nervous spell he was under broke. Suddenly, he turned to me and said, "Elizabeth, what do you do?" Translation: why are you here and why are you credible?

Without knowing what I had done, I smiled and answered curtly, "I'm the author of two books, with a third on the way, and I have a radio show."

This bruised his ego. In academia, success is measured only two ways: being published and being tenured. I didn't give thought to that when I responded. It appeared to him that I pushed my accomplishments in his face, and I had most definitely brought my A game. My silence and his talking made him lose power. At some point, he knew that and thought to ask who I was in the room. My swift remark made a strong statement. Basically, I punched him in the dick.

A few minutes later the conference leader informed him that I would be speaking for forty-five minutes, and he would be speaking for fifteen. Again, I didn't notice the significance of this, and to my amazement he was outraged and had a small outburst. Clearly, I stepped on his toes by standing three feet from him.

The lesson? Be the expert, but know your audience. Experts are taken more seriously than novices. It's a fine balance to be credible and not hurt another with your accomplishments.

Men get insecure as well. Be astute, intuitive, and sensitive.

Chapter 6

Lack of Confidence

"The problem is not with life. The problem is you haven't taken charge of your mind."—Sadguru, Isha Foundation

I always take questions at the end of my talks. One woman sitting in the back said, "Elizabeth, I attended one of your talks recently, and you told us about the monkey in our heads. That really helped me. Can you tell that story again?"

Your mind is like a monkey. It goes from thought to thought for hours on end. It rattles on so much, we often don't have any idea about what is going on up there. In fact, we often think we are our thoughts. We think "I AM ANGRY" or "I AM HAPPY," but none of that is true. You are not your thoughts. You identify with the thought, and that is the problem. The problem is not stopping the thought, either, which has been a common thread in the "mindfulness" books on the market during the last fifteen years. *It is impossible to stop your mind.*

The monkey is the thought.

Each thought runs wild like a monkey swinging from branch to branch. If it is not monitored, your monkey (thoughts) will go wild. Consider your mind the cage and your thoughts the monkey, who runs from thing to thing, never satisfied. The monkey runs *you.*

What do you suppose a monkey left unattended does?

Answer: it throws poo and bananas all over the cage. You don't want your mind like that, do you? Do you want your mind and eventually your life (which reflects your mind) to be a total stinky mess?

No, of course not.

So, don't feed the monkeys in your head. It's your job to not feed the monkeys, and it's a full-time job, without weekends off, no holidays, no smoke breaks, no time off for good behavior. Mind your mind, or someone else will. Likely it will be your monkey that takes possession of your mind.

For women, the monkey is the thought that tells you that you are fat or ugly, or not smart enough, or don't have good ideas at work. All of us have monkeys, but it's an interesting process to slow down enough to see the monkeys and to start to disassociate from your mind. Trust me, I've done this with a lot of success. Women's monkeys are very damaging in the cage. Your monkey perpetuates every false idea you've ever had about yourself.

Oh, and one other thing, in case you haven't noticed: *the monkey always lies.*

The problem is twofold: you don't know that you have monkeys (bad thoughts), and you don't know you are feeding them (by believing your mind and making that story your identity), and therefore buying into the lies.

You are not your thoughts.

Therefore, you must never feed the monkey.

The mind is jumping about, like an animal, piddling on the floor, jumping from thing to thing, and basically out of control. Until it's harnessed and one makes friends with their mind, they are a slave to circumstances, most of which started within the vain components of the mind, before it manifested into reality. Women fall into victimhood easily. All of us do it, actually; many a powerful person I've met at work had a mind that worked overtime and caused them a lot of agony.

Fear is nothing but a product your mind creates.

Dianne came to me for coaching. At fifty-one, she was well accomplished and made a sizeable income until she was laid off. During that time her father died, and it was extremely difficult for her. To pull herself up by her bootstraps and recover from the shock of being let go, coupled with the death of a parent, she went back to school for an MBA. Two years ticked by, then three. With her education in hand, she started looking for another role, insisting that she receive the same pay. Frankly, she was worth every penny; however, her mind wreaked havoc. She worried she wouldn't find another job. It took all she could muster to network, apply for jobs, and go to job interviews and risk being rejected. She had no idea that her mind played a big factor into her current reality.

The homework I gave her for a week was to wake up and instantly see how quickly she began to think. Most importantly, to look at her thoughts. What went on up there the moment her eyes opened and she landed in her body?

Few of us know exactly what goes on in our minds. Think about that carefully. Things that you wanted, or worse, didn't want, all started in your mind. Nothing comes of nothing.

I boldly stated on a recent radio show that even a small thought can ruin your life. Thoughts have major power, I emphasized. My cohost challenged me on this, and I answered, "Think about that. Even a divorce starts with a thought. Nothing comes of nothing. Your first thought was, 'My husband is a total jerk.' That sets up a pattern. Soon you are in a courthouse with lawyers around tying up loose ends."

The confidence gap in women isn't a feeling or a hunch. In a woman's mind, it's very real.

Here is how a lack of confidence manifests:

- Studies show that men initiate salary negotiations four times as often as women
- When a woman asks for money, she asks for an amount 30 percent less than what men request. (NY Times, Jan 2016 "Bridging the Pay Gap")

Shockingly, men tend to overestimate their abilities and performance, *while women underestimate both.*

Bottom line: women don't have confidence to negotiate a decent salary, even if they are well educated and have held the leadership title. In fact, I've had women clients with director titles who got their stomachs tied up in knots thinking about negotiating the next salary level. This shocks me. How did they get that far and yet are afraid to talk about money?

What I found was a big difference between men and women. For example, if I was coaching a man who was in transition, in the first session, he'd bravely lean over the table at Starbucks and ask, "You know the market. How much can I get? I made $150,000 on the base. Should I ask for $160,000? $170,000?"

Recently my reply to that question was, "Gee, how much do you need?" This comment tends to be a reality check for a greedy man. Really, how much is enough? If you need it because you have two kids in college, that's a different story. More isn't always better. You should give up more time for more money, and few men see that immediately. If you are just asking me what the market will bear, I can tell you that as well.

In contrast, women I coach will not mention money or their salary, ever. I have to bring it up. Every time. Women are focused on the job search, and typically were tortured by a "bad" boss or are unemployed. By the third session I mention salary, and it usually goes like this: "Did you know that you are underpaid by $20,000?"

Shocked, the women look at me and say, "No. Are you sure? I would have known. I'm not sure I could really ask for that much more when interviewing."

Why on earth NOT?

During that third session, these capable women confess in hushed whispers that they feared something was "wrong with them," and they really wanted my help to teach them confidence. Frankly, I was dumbfounded. Many were highly educated and accomplished, and made over six figures, and yet they deeply doubted themselves. How could this even be?

I distinctly remember a few years ago hiring a female vice president for a client-facing operations role. During the final steps of the process, I called her to ensure she wanted the job and to ask her how much she wanted to make, since we were about to sharpen our pencils and put together an offer. I made it clear the next call I would make to her would be with an offer extended. What ensued was a weird conversation that went like this: "Well, I don't know. I want what is fair, but I don't want to leave money on the table. I'm sure you can come up with something fair, because I honestly don't know."

This floored me. How does a woman with *a MBA in finance* not know her market worth? Worse, why was this conversation so painful and difficult? It was embarrassing for me to witness her stumbling around and basically telling me that I can offer her anything and she would take it, which was a big, fat lie.

I handled it by replying, "That isn't true. You wouldn't take anything, would you? Let's do this. Let's play with some numbers. Take out a calculator. How much did you make on your base salary? Forget the bonus, that's window dressing. Okay...do you want to make a 5 percent increase? Ten percent? Fifteen?"

I literally walked her through a negotiation, and she finally realized how ridiculous this was and became somewhat ashamed. I promised her I would never share this with the executives and that the conversation was just between us. After calculating the numbers, she knew immediately that even a 10 percent increase was not enough, but she did want the job. Even a woman who seems to have it all can be short on confidence when it comes to her own earnings.

Confidence is something that is built, like a muscle, over time.

There is an art to quiet confidence, and it is never prettier than when it is worn by a woman. You know her when you see her at a meeting in the office. She is understated, yet powerful. Her silence is presence enough. She doesn't have to fill the room with noise. When she speaks, people listen and take her council. She doesn't compete. She reports information, she collaborates, and she knows how to work alone and within a team and is extremely careful about her political capital.

Political capital—yes, you read that correctly.

Political capital is critical and this concept was taught to me by a Director, named Neil Prater. With more value than street cred, political capital can be earned and burned. Like real money, political capital is earned from others. It comes from the consensus that a person is on point. Consistency earns her this currency, and over time she becomes wealthy through popular demand. Don't be fooled—just as money is earned and lost, so is political capital. It can be lost and feel like the biggest recession of your life. Women who have capital attract many people who want to align with her. Some want what she can provide—stability, a good salary, and popularity. Others flock to her because they believe she has a message they can get behind. Some need her for protection. Some need her power.

No woman ever obtained political capital from dressing a certain way or from being nice or from popularity. She earns it from being steady and consistent. She's read the boy's book of code rules in the office and gets it. She knows she is a capable player, and she never lets them see her sweat. Men respect her, and over time these same men will ask her privately for her suggestions or point of view, but she never lets this get to her head. One dance with her own ego will allow her to slip. She has earned her seat at the table to play with the big boys.

She would never dream of competing with other women, because she knows that will blow back on her and her political currency will diminish. In addition, she knows men hate that sort of behavior. She is invited to a seat at the table and continues to earn that right, never taking it for granted. She attends and sometimes even orchestrates the meeting before the meeting.

If she must make an unfavorable call and side against the popular vote in the office, she is willing to burn some of the political capital. She is not a "yes (wo)man," which is another reason why she is so respected at work.

If she is the only female in a position of power and is surrounded by men, she knows she needs to get into the boys' club immediately. There is no beating them; there is only joining them.

The three words that sum up this woman are: consistent (emotionally), trusted, and competent.

Are you?

If you think you fall short in the confidence department, don't worry; many of us do.

Many women come to me and ask me to specifically teach them how to be confident. I can't do that. *All confidence comes from within.* You'll have to wrestle with your own thoughts, break them down, see where they came from, and throw the limiting thoughts out. Once you feel even a little bit confident, you'll trust yourself. Once you trust yourself to bail yourself out of situations, the confidence will grow.

Below are a few exercises you can try for one week to build confidence:

Exercise # 1

Stay away from media or limit your cyber time. This includes TV, Facebook, and other social platforms. Get your face out of your phone. Go on a media diet for a short period of time. The media has dozens of messages in an hour that colors a women in an unfavorable light. Over time, this affects our perception. You wouldn't drink poison, so why would you spend fifteen hours a week watching TV or surfing the Net? Mind your mind. See what's up there.

Exercise #2

Cultivate the disposition to do the things you hate doing. For example, if you hate drinking water and prefer Diet Coke, drink water. While that seems small, it's the smallest things we resist doing that sabotage ourselves. Cultivate not caring what you like or don't like. Just do the right thing, repeatedly. If that is too big of a stretch, just notice how many times in one single hour you find you don't "like" something. Doing this squashes fear inside you, diminishes ego (thinking "I" and "Mine"), and builds discipline. Over time you are poised. You know why? You begin to trust yourself.

Exercise #3

Look at what you tell yourself. The most important habit a person can get into is watching their thoughts. Thoughts are not real. They are nothing at all unless you attach to them. Try it. When you wake up in the morning, what is the first thought in your head? Pay attention. This is where the root of insecurity lies, in your mind.

Exercise #4

Don't gather more information. Do something. I had a female client who would sit in session with me, go home and read stuff online, talk to her friends, and then come back to me to ask me if what we were doing was right, because she took in so much information. It made no sense to me. She paid for a professional to guide her, and now she is clouding her mind. Stick to the program, I told her. Many of us read volumes of self-help books, but fail to implement one small concept. In fact, most of your "problem" is believing something is wrong with you. There is *nothing* wrong with you. Believing that thought leads to more insecurities.

And finally, let it go. Whatever your ex-husband, boyfriend, father, or boss told you that really hurt you deep inside is nothing but a festering pack of lies. Believing what everyone said about you starts a victim mentality mindset. Victims run from situation to situation to validate that they are...what? Victims!

Let go of every false belief you've ever had about yourself.

Chapter 7

Mean Girls

Plaid for Women is an online magazine that I've written articles for about leadership and work. Sarah Zink and I do a monthly radio show called, "Leadership Lessons from the Lioness." Plaid for Women is a powerful and thought-provoking conglomerate of women. Our motto is: We are about the business of life. My contribution is on leadership, work, and business.

A year ago, Plaid for Women tripped and fell into a concept that rang true for me and many other women: Shivaun Palmer, the CEO, brought up the term "mean girls", from the movie entitled the same with Lindsay Lohan - and it stuck. Her mission was to identify and make ourselves aware of the mean girl that hides in every one of us. Plaid for Women started a campaign called "No Mean Girls," which included articles, radio shows, and videos around the concept. With one thousand women, a month signing up for online membership, I'd say they are onto something. Unless we let go of the mean girl within us, we will never be able to rise into position of power, nor be taken seriously. Every day we see examples of mean girls at work.

Alicia Morgan, a blogger for Plaid for Women, said it best in an article entitled, "Understanding Of Mean Girls" Her article boiled it down to five simple reasons; all of which, I believe, are worth contemplation:

   1. **The Me Factor**. Mean girls must be the center of attention at all times. Competition is heavy, and only one rock star can exist.

2. **Mean Girls Hurt**. Mean girls are in pain themselves and lash out. Recently I read a post online stating that defensiveness is actually a person screaming out to be respected. Mean girls project that uncomfortable energy onto another in the hope of getting rid of it.

3. **Insecurity**. A mean girl will attack anyone who has something she secretly wants, but doesn't know how to get herself.

4. **Need to Discredit**. Mean girls will discredit another to get ahead. This stems from items number three and number two, discussed above.

5. **"No" to Sisterhood**. Mean girls don't like to be "joiners" or to collaborate; being alone is how they gain power. They mask this by saying that their directness is just fine and other women don't accept their "honesty." Their brand of "honesty" is a shit sandwich wrapped up and packaged as something else.

The No Mean Girls concept has great value if we want to be taken seriously in business and get ahead. How can we as women climb to the top if we don't support and promote each other? Sarah asked me on a recent show if we as women should reach out to another woman when we see her stumble in a meeting, by giving her feedback. My response: it's not a good idea, because reaching out may be misconstrued as you are judging her. Until we get our own backyards cleaned up, there is no reason to overstep and give what we think is helpful criticism.

There is a mean girl in all of us, and after reviewing the above list, I see that most often in my own life I fall into category number five. Although I have never openly lashed out or excluded other women, I did often say "no" to sisterhood, again and again. It occurred to me about four years ago that this may be hurting me and my career, and when I shrank back and recoiled at the thought of sisterhood, I purposely took a hard look at myself. What was it about joining a party that made me so hesitant?

While my wiring is not to be a joiner, I think it's a fine line. Joining every cause can lead one to be overwhelmed. Having your own voice is important, too. Marching to only the beat of your drum can cause isolation and separation. No one likes "bossy, bossy. apple saucy women." There is a place for leading. There is also a place for following and getting along. The trick, which I eventually mastered, is knowing what to do in each situation.

The longer I live, the more I see that it is never "this" or "that," it's a lot of "and." "This AND that" can also be true in the same moment.

As I pointed out in Chapter 3, being a woman means being biologically programmed to be competitive to land the best male to breed and reproduce. Today this no longer necessary for survival.

I believe we can overcome being mean girls.

Furthermore, I have overcome (for the most part) being a mean girl. Isolation is no longer my drug of choice.

We can do this by first seeing where we are a mean girl. It's easy to point out when we as women have been snubbed by another woman. But can we see where *we* are the problem? Do you catch yourself being a mean girl in the office? Are you big enough to pull that woman aside and openly apologize?

Often, we read things and don't think they apply to **us.** For example, take the expression, "Be the change you want the world to become." Great concept. Very thought provoking, but when you read that, do you think, "How can I be better?" No, we often think it's about everyone else. Everyone else needs to feed the poor, be more compassionate, stop being greedy and stop being selfish. The list of our judgments of others goes on and on, while we never see how we contribute to the problem.

I'll never forget the day that I wrote an email to my teacher, when I wrote in the subject line, "I AM THE PROBLEM." That was five short years ago. The epiphany that I, myself, could be adding a pile of hurt onto the ones I love the most (specifically, my husband), as well as polluting the world with my thoughts was, frankly, shocking. Here I thought I had it all together. I realized I not only did NOT have it together but I was also causing a ton of damage. The body count and wreckage behind me was staggering. Once I really got it, I cried. Openly, I wept for all my small sins that were so huge to me. I saw what I had done and what I had failed to do: apologize. I looked at the years of hurt I caused coworkers, old bosses, my ex-husband, my deceased family, my current husband, and his family. The list seemed to be endless, yet I never gave into self-loathing. I just looked and witnessed. The walls of separation were being broken down in my psyche, and I wondered what would happen if I let my vain illusion of my ego go. My ego, which told me who I was and that I was right. I knew that isolation would no longer keep me safe. If I let that concept go, who would I become? What would I become?

Knowing that I was the problem was overwhelming. Once that settled a bit, I saw how the smallest things I said hurt others. I saw how my actions were driven by thinking that others didn't appreciate my frankness when in reality, I hurt a lot of people. Many think that is just being a 'strong woman', but it's not. It's

58

really being a bitch. The fact was I had believed my own lies, fed my own monkey and shoved the responsibility off to everyone around me, thinking they weren't tough enough to take my feedback. Those around me were the weak ones who couldn't stomach my direct nature and I saw others as the problem. The mask I wore to the world was slipping off. I saw there was little power in being alone. Mostly I saw how everything I said and did created an impression. Worse, it LEFT an impression.

"Everything touches everything," the sage told me. "You are not separate. You think you are separate, but you are not. Minimally air connects all of you."

Followed by, "Intention is the name of the game. It's the most important part. What is behind what you are saying and doing?" Those words, sent to me in an email, gave me a lot to think about, for weeks. Truth is a stubborn thing; it stands the test of time. The common denominator was always me.

Occasionally, you get a privilege in life. It happens with such obvious force, that you know immediately when you recognize a woman who isn't a mean girl. It's her behavior that makes you want to be a better person.

Carolyn was my opportunity—she was my grand situation. The situation to beat all situations, and for which I am eternally and heartfelt drop-to-my-knees grateful.

Carolyn Suero was my best friend, and I lost track of her after my entire family died. One could say I was a little preoccupied burying both of my brothers, my mother and grandmother within four short years. The oddest part is that no one in my extended family helped during the crisis. I literally was responsible for holding my family members' hands when they died, and for cleaning out their apartments of their earthly possessions. To this day I'm not sure why no one stepped up and helped. Carolyn was my best friend and there throughout this insurmountable time in my life.

With no time to grieve myself, I kept moving. It was the only thing I knew how to do. I'll never forget my first husband screaming at me in an argument that no one cared that my family was dead. As cruel as it was, *he was right*.

Here was the AND statement: no one cared AND I could choose to suck it up and move on with my life without it destroying me. Both were true.

What I didn't realize was when I moved on, Carolyn was left in my tail lights.

There is a funny expression that you must give up everything in order to gain everything, and that is exactly what happened to me. Having my family ripped away gave me huge freedom in life, but through the grief at that time, I didn't know that. As I grew older, and as I write these very pages, I am grateful for not being so attached to everything, including family, which can be a real illusion set up for disappointment. I come before you with no entanglements. Through that lack, I became full within myself.

Death taught me what a bad day really was in life and not to whine about the ups and downs. Death taught me all things end, including the vain notion of myself. Death taught me the beauty of transition and that endings were not only okay, but a good thing. But the greatest gift was my teacher, whom I lovingly call the sage, who showed up in my life. He taught me death wasn't an ending at all, and that life was, in fact, a process. Even bigger than that, he taught me that *I* was a process.

I met Carolyn in high school, but I can't remember where exactly. I think we had a class together and I sat in front of her, but I could be wrong. She occupied every thought I had and shared every laugh and tear I shed until I was 22 and left for the west coast. I told her every secret, every close portion of my heart and mind, and she shared the same with me. Years later she confided I was the only person that she allowed over to her house, which stunned me. I wondered why I was chosen. It was a mutual friendship that grew into a deep bond that words can't really explain.

Losing track of me was painful for her, and I had no idea of that as I floated through my own life. For years, Carolyn would dream about me. In each dream, we were reunited. I was the unresolved person for her, and she found her mind wondering, what ever happened to Elizabeth? Where is she?

After two decades, one weekend afternoon I found a private message on Facebook from Carolyn. She was extremely respectful and said that she certainly didn't mean to intrude in any way; she had been looking for me for twenty-three years. "Looking for me" may have been an understatement: she tirelessly hunted for me for countless years to no avail, until that one June evening.

I read the Facebook post and was stunned.

After all these years. What would I say?

The message hit while I was sitting at lunch with my husband, and for a while I didn't know how I felt about any of it. Carolyn was the *only* link to my past. There was no family. There was no one who knew me from back then and, honestly, I liked my clean life. I enjoyed and reveled in having no history and no trace.

There is something freeing about not having a past and having no connections. You can be who you are with no reference points. You can grow and no one can remember you when you did something stupid or unsavory. The pain, hurts, tears, and fears can remain yours and yours alone. It's privacy at its best, and now being in the public eye, I have learned to crave privacy. My favorite guilty pleasure is walking into Starbucks with tattered yoga pants on and a sweat shirt and being anonymous. My profession as a writer allows me that privacy. Inviting Carolyn back in would be inviting back in the past, someone who knew me more intimately than anyone. Even my dead family didn't know me like she did. Would she judge me? Would she be impressed by who I was today? And, really, why did I care about that anyway?

So, I sat with those thoughts for a while before I responded to her. Here it was again, the tendency to go it alone, the pull to not join a sisterhood. But I couldn't do it with Carolyn, and I knew that having her back would not open a Pandora's box of pain within me, because I had cried all I could cry and moved on. To some people's amazement, I had moved on a little bit too much. I distinctly remember my father before he died, and how he was a little angry that I did move on with my life, and that the family's passing never defined me, while he wallowed in the pain of both his sons' untimely deaths. As I sat in hospice with my father before his passing, he said very little to me. In fact, his only statement was looking me directly in the eye and saying, "It couldn't have been easy."

There, in a setting called hospice, was the approval I craved my entire life. Freedom rooted in me the moment he died and for that, I was grateful.

I pushed all my ego aside, let go of all the crap in my head and called Carolyn, and we talked for five hours. Within three months

I boarded a plane to see her and meet her two kids. Her husband I already knew, because I was there the day they met. That's how far and how deep I go back with Carolyn.

She looked the same as she did in high school. Life hadn't hardened her. In fact, life had made her deeper and softer, which was amazing to witness. It was an eerie feeling that no time had separated us at all, and yet, here was a grown woman whom I didn't know. I didn't know her as an adult, or of her hopes and fears. I didn't know her as a mother, or as of a woman who ran a nonprofit and had given her entire life to service. I loved the girl I knew in high school, but it was such a pleasure to get to know the women she had become, and to find to my utter surprise there were no pauses in the conversation, no hidden agendas, no secrets left to unfold. This is someone who, had I met her in another setting, I would certainly give her my phone number and invite her to coffee to yak.

Not once did I feel a trace of competition with Carolyn.

There was no comparing our lives with each other; there was no nosy sense of wondering whether her life was better than mine or vice versa. It was clear we both had vastly different paths: mine was simple for the most part, full of exploring, moving, working, and being able to turn on a dime, while Carolyn rooted deeply—at work, with family, and at home. Thank God she did root, because otherwise she never would have found me.

The movie *Blood Brother* reminded me of us and of the deep bond that words would cheapen if I tried to explain. In the documentary, one friend goes to India and has a crazy life, and can never go back to Pennsylvania. He knows it, and so does everyone else. His heart is in service for children with AIDS in India in an orphanage, and he continues his life there. The other friend stays in Philly, but never loses track of the other. The friendship is as deep as brothers, and possibly deeper. Both live very different lives, but this thick bond that can't be broken, nor explained. Even with two continents between them, they are connected. They laugh and they cry. There is a karmic dance, perhaps even a debt the two of them have with each other that has to play out, and it does play out, beautifully.

Being reunited with Carolyn unearthed deep feelings of love, acceptance, and friendship. The whispers and secrets we had back then led to baring our souls as adult women. Conversations around our marriages, our guilt, our joy, our families, and work. I still love her deeply. To this day I cannot believe that anyone on this earth looked for me as long and as hard as she did, and I am extremely humbled by the thought. There was plenty of opportunity for uncles, aunts, and cousins to check in with me over the years or invite me to a holiday dinner. No invitations came, but Carolyn never gave up. In some way, I haunted her.

Carolyn is not a mean girl. Never has been and never will be a mean girl. She was a testimonial to me that we as woman can also have that soft side. She gave me the gift of opportunity to be transparent and vulnerable. I took that gift and grew immeasurably.

Witnessing Carolyn's life humbles me in many ways. I could never do what she does in life. In fact, I know if I were given her life, I'd be a hot mess. I don't think I have the personality or inclination to rise to the occasions that present themselves in any given day in Carolyn's life. Watching how she navigates situations is staggering to me, and if I think about it too much, I start to get so humbled, I cry. It's an honor to be her friend, and witness her life, especially after all these years.

Reuniting with Carolyn made me see the value of never being a mean girl again.

The visit was more than reuniting with an old friend. It gave me the wisdom to see that isolation isn't power. Isolation is a silly notion that the mind creates and enforces ego. I've learned that competition is a dark shadow that leaves one alone.

Never again will I say "no" to sisterhood.

Chapter 8

Words that Diminish Credibility

Perceptions.

Those things that form quickly, and set to be as immovable as cement. Blind spots are a lack of awareness of the impression you leave on others. You think you are just having a conversation, or making a post on social media, but just outside your view, opinions are being instantly formed about you.

Language, our primary form of communication, is part of the bedrock of our culture and everyday life. The written word started out as a sacred tool. To this day, countries divide or unify through treaties, while business covenants "marry" or "divorce" companies through meetings, and later, contracts.

Relationships are formed or broken over spoken words. Consider that everything you say - or don't say – has a responsibility and an affect. And yet, we women are often unable to see how the words we use daily in the office can affect perceptions.

These are small, insidious ways women discredit themselves repeatedly:

Apologizing: "I'm sorry. I'm sorry." What are you sorry about? Constant apologizing can be the kiss of death for a woman in the office. Unless you ran into someone's car, there is no reason to be constantly sorry.

Why we do this: Women do this in the office because somewhere along the line they were brought up to have good manners, but in this scenario, it backfires. Other women do this because they feel they are overly accountable for everything, thus the incessant need to apologize. Saying "Excuse me" in some situations would fare better than saying "Sorry." Women who constantly say they are sorry leave the impression that they are weak, particularly to men. Men never do this. Have you ever seen a CEO give poor earnings publicly and say on camera, "I'm sorry, but we didn't hit our earnings as planned." No, because it's absurd. And for a woman to say she is sorry for no reason is equally preposterous.

Asking Questions You Know Already the Answers to: I call this "up speak." It's when women end sentences with questions, on purpose, to keep the dialogue going. Silence is powerful. Be okay with sitting in it, especially at meetings. If you know you get nervous and start talking too much, focus on your breath: watch it rise and fall in your chest. Disengage the wild thoughts and the compulsion.

Why we do this: Women do this for two main reasons, based on my observations. The first is they hate silence, and they feel the need to fill it. This can be caused from a bad case of nerves. The second reason they do this to be collaborative. Women have a deep need to be included and to include others, but in this scenario, it backfires. Remember, the office is full of men. You don't want to be perceived as the woman who talks too much with little substance to her words.

Wishy-Washy Speak: Nothing on earth discredits a woman (especially with a man in a meeting) than words like: perhaps, just, actually, maybe, a little bit, etc. Be definite in your speech. You are not "a little bit concerned" with your disruptive employee. State instead that you are concerned. The bottom line is, you are so concerned, you are trying to figure out a way to fire them! No one in the room feels comfortable with "maybe" or a "little bit" of anything. Be firm. Be definite. Have an opinion—it's okay.

Why we do this: Women do this indirect speak to soften the blow. They have a difficult time speaking the truth in fear of hurting the other person. Again, this behavior stems from a beautiful place, but backfires in the office. The perception left behind is that the woman is indecisive, and in business, being decisive is everything.

Fear of Being a Woman: Many times, I've been asked if I had to "act more like a man" to get ahead in business. Never. This isn't about changing who you are or asking you to shelf being sensitive, compassionate, and collaborative. Find your voice and style. Women can be very powerful and not come off being authoritative or bitchy.

Why we do this: Women are very conflicted. They have a fear of being perceived as masculine, and have notions of what it would look like to take a position of power in the office. Although a woman is conflicted and doesn't want to trade her feminine qualities for a promotion, she also desires that type of power. She is trapped in either-or thinking. *Either* I can act like a man and get ahead, *or* I should stay in a support role. I can't have both. There is no room for both. Overall, her fear of being a woman is really about her fear of being called a bitch. She struggles with being direct but not too direct. She struggles with being taught the value of being the nice girl, sugar and spice and everything nice, that's was little girls are made of. This backfires in the office, because men can smell this and concluded that you don't have confidence.

Here's what it boils down to at work:

Like it or not, men rule the world in business. If that weren't true, we'd see more than 5 percent of women placed as CEOs in the market. There is a game that is being played in the office. Know there is a game and figure out the rules and boundaries. Once you get the game, play.

As a woman in leadership manage and monitor your perceptions in the office. It's critical to your success.

Chapter 9

How to Get Invited into the Boys' Club

Before we launch into this next concept, I think it's important to define what the boys' club is.

Urban Dictionary (http://www.urbandictionary.com/define.php?term=boys+club defines the "boys club") as:

> 1. A group of men that when together act like boys; joking around and goofing around with each other.

> 2. A term for an [sic] club that only allows men into their group. Often used as a way to get away from their wives/girlfriends and hang out with other like-minded individuals.

As I discussed in previous chapters, we can understand why men don't want us in their club in the office. Managing our perceptions is key, but getting invited into the boys' club, no matter how stupid you might think that is, can be a critical factor. It's the adage: if you can't beat them, join them.

Ultimately, one day the topic will be leadership, not "female leadership," and I believe the fundamental breakdown is OUR breakdown as women. It's time to break down all the false notions we've had about ourselves, each other, men, and even the boys' club. Unity is ultimately the principal to bridge diversity, and it starts in the mind.

Professional women are on a tightrope when it comes to work. Speak up too much, and we are labeled aggressive. Speak too little in a meeting with men, and we are labeled as too passive. It's the delicate balance of listening and speaking.

Years ago, I desperately wanted into the boys' club, but didn't know how to get in. My husband suggested that I learned how to talk sports, which immediately made me feel inadequate. The problem was I had no interest in sports and knew nothing about it. My husband told me that I didn't have to watch Monday Night Football or subscribe to a sports channel. I just needed to know the headlines. Most men watch football, so I picked that as my target, and each night I read some headline about an all-star player. Ironically, I found it akin to following a soap opera. Players had personal lives that blew up around them, making them vulnerable to the press. It seemed like there was always something to talk about, but I did have to keep up on the stories that unfolded. Total time investment was about twenty minutes a day, just reading headlines and asking my husband questions if I stumbled across something I didn't understand.

What I found was astonishing. Weaving in subtle comments into conversations made me very intriguing to executives, and using sports analogies within business made me down-right amazing.

Here's an example of how to use simple sports talk to move into unity awareness.

> Me: Hey, didn't you grow up in Philadelphia? I thought you mentioned that at lunch.
>
> Director: Yeah, I did.
>
> Me: I heard that the Philadelphia Eagles have a jail in the stadium so that rowdy fans get arrested and automatically booked right then and there. Did you ever see a game in that stadium?
>
> Director: Oh yeah, I've been to many games. Love it. It's always cold as hell, too, but that doesn't keep the fans down. Yeah, we have a jail. You know the judge really

made it big time when he opened that jail. Got written up all over the place. We are the only NFL team that has that, which is surprising. You'd think the Raiders would have their own jail since most of their fans are gang members that sit in the Black Hole.

Okay, if you are reading this and you don't know what the Black Hole is or where the Raiders hail from, then you are in the dust. I had this little conversation in front of one other woman and two other men. Instantly, this little tidbit created huge sense of unity between the director and myself. To be totally transparent, this little factoid was something I picked up years ago listening to my husband, and I found it shocking and interesting. Hedging my bets that this director would want to hail from the land of the toughest team, I threw it out there. Fishing expedition well done.

I don't need to know the quarterback of every team. I don't need to know the score of last night's game. To this day, I still have no interest in sports, but I can bridge a gap and set myself apart from any preconceived notion about women in an office.

Here's another example of creating coloration by using sport analogies. This conversation happened through IM (instant message)

> Me: I've been blocking for you all day long so you could run with the ball. Do you know I had three meetings this week alone around your open position? Everyone is looking at it and if we don't pull the trigger, you may lose the requisition entirely.
>
> Director: I know. I need to sit down and think about it. There were good candidates.
>
> Me: Please give me an answer by tomorrow morning. I can't keep the shoulder pads on forever, you know. I'm

standing in front of them and they are about to mow you down.

Director: Yes, first thing in the morning, I'll have an answer. Thanks for doing that. What did you think of Tom?

Look at the language I used. Words like "blocking" and "shoulder pads" conjure up the image that I am at war for the director. The sports analogy tells him I'm on the same team, and we are together, yet I never lost my footing in the conversation. I closed with asking for an answer and reminding him he is lucky to have me on his side, and in the end, he asked for my opinion.

This is when you know that you are "in" and not on the outside looking in.

Another way to relate is to do what I never had the guts to do - take up golf. I am a total spaz when it comes to sports, which is probably why I have no interest in them. Gym class was a painful memory for me. Let's put it this way, I got picked last for dodge ball and was the first person out. That's how bad I was. There was no way I could muster up any kind of courage to learn golf since I nearly maimed my husband during round of miniature golf when my club nearly met his face when I put some gusto into my swing. However, if you are brave enough, this is a great game to learn. Lessons for beginners and for women-only are available in case you just can't stomach learning with a mixed group. I've come across a few women in sales who learned the game, and it panned out well for them, financially.

Getting into the boys' club is about learning a common language. This can be a challenge for women who work in male-dominated professions or fields such as accounting, insurance, and financial services. If are you surrounded by a male-dominated industry, it's even more vital to your success that you bridge the communication gap.

I think that women at work do it differently. We talk about our kids or our families at work with other women. We talk about feelings or things that are personal to create a bond. Men bond through play, not pain, and that is a key difference.

Give it a try: find a way to bond and bridge a gap with the men in your office.

Chapter 10

Letting Go of Your Story

There seems to be a new trend, called "telling your story," and I don't like it at all. I question whether this is really a good practice for women. In the 1980s on women's talk shows, I think it did serve a powerful purpose, but lately I think it reeks of weakness. A quick Google search told me that there were forty thousand articles on women's leadership, and a whopping fifty-six thousand on storytelling. Clearly there is a trend, but I've never been a trend follower. Here's my stance: question trends; question the status quo. Just because everyone is doing it, doesn't make it right or good.

My biggest concern is that if there really is a woman's movement toward leadership and success, telling our stories will only leave us stuck in our past.

It is the mind telling you that you aren't enough. All of us have had a horrible time in our lives when something traumatic occurred, either due to circumstance or something internal that went wrong. We all have had devastating childhoods, marriages, whatever it is...fill in the blank. Some days we think the pain will never end, and we know somewhere deep inside we are spinning and we can't stop. We don't think we can change it and we feel powerless.

When your trauma defines your life and becomes your story, it's a problem. Don't kid yourself that by sharing you are helping another. Likely you are fishing for sympathy or some emotional response that will continue the charge.

It sounds odd, but people get an electrical charge and get to relive the trauma by talking about it. It's a farce to think that sharing painful memories will heal them. It only reopens the wound, and sharing doesn't help anyone else out. What's really in it for someone to listen to another's woes? Nothing. The person telling the story gets the payoff, not the listener. I'm not saying don't talk through things when you hurt; I'm simply stating, don't let the hurts define you.

It takes a person to relate to a situation to create a victim. Nothing is really happening to YOU. It's just happening. Some psychological therapies hold that talking about it, whatever it is, helps. Talking about it, though, perpetuates the victim. There are very few people I've known who went to a therapist and got dramatically better. Most people that I know who did talk therapy uncovered more and more things that were wrong with them. It is an endless cycle, leaving people in therapy for years and thousands of dollars spent with little or no relief. The more I look at psychology, in my opinion, it is based on a dualist model: there is YOU, and there is the PROBLEM. What we should do is look at how we relate to what's going *on outside* of us. How you relate to it is everything. How you see it is everything. Orientation is the name of the game. Attitude and approach. It starts with you.

It's very easy to point at everyone and everything else. I remember the day I realized that I was the common dominator to everything in my life. This ideology forces a person inside of themselves, and if you look inside, the victim can't exist, and over time, neither can the story. If you are getting angry just reading this chapter, then I've poked at the crying little girl victim within you. This is a good thing; she'll fight, struggle, kick, and scream to stay alive.

Our "story" gets set up for us when we were children. We are taught that if we work hard, we will be rewarded. This sets up a dangerous pattern. We are first taught to get good grades in school, then we are taught to go to the best college, and perhaps even encouraged to find a mate. Then we are told to get the best job possible. And a house. Have children, and if anything along the way happens that is unpleasant, well, that is a horrible thing to contend with.

We are not taught that the actual shit show part of our lives should be a *welcomed* experience, because it's in the horror, agony, and pain is where we really get to grow. Life really is how you see it and how you process it. Even the big things that hit you.

For example, cancer can be a great growth opportunity. You'll learn you aren't the body.

Job loss can be a real ego crusher, but you will find out you are more than your work and your money.

Divorce; weight gain; growing old; having pain; being rejected; failure are all grand opportunities in this school called life. If you run into those situations rather than shrink from them, you will find opportunity. Poking around for sympathy and consolation is not the way to conduct your life, because it will set you up as the victim. You'll be a puppet on a string, walking around and reacting to everything in your mind and everything outside that you label as "bad".

Few of us understand that *this is life*.

It's possible that horrible things happen. You could say your prayers every night, and your son could get killed on the way to the store. You could go to the doctors with a lump in your breast and survive chemotherapy. You could lose your job after twenty years. Sad fact is, our parents don't set us up for this, and in return, we didn't raise our kids with this notion, either.

These things will happen, and when they do, we think we are the ONLY people who have had it happen to us. *Our pain makes us special.*

"Special" thinking sets us up for victimhood. We can't see it, we don't know it, and we are suddenly there, looking for an audience, a friend, anyone who might listen to our pain and give us some reprieve. Then we wonder why we don't feel relief after we've told our sad stories.

My personal issue with women telling their stories is about what story telling does to them. Typically, it reemphasizes the pain.

You are not a victim.

You are not your pain.

Let's face it, it's very easy to allow situations in life to take over us and our emotions. It's actually very hard to stand up and decide that we have a choice in how we look at situations, and draw the line when it comes to having the situation define us.

I know pain.

I understand pain.

These words that I write are coming from a person who buried her entire family. By the time I was twenty-one my entire family died. Can you imagine that? Having your entire family dead, being responsible for burying them, and you haven't even finished college yet? I remember the moment I had to decide to stop the spiral of self-pity and move on with my life. It was a defining moment because it was much easier to wallow in my story of pain. In fact, this is the first time I've ever publicly stated that my family is dead. It's a story I never tell, to anyone. *Ever.*

Because no one cares.

And because telling that story will set up a horrific charge in my mind and body, and I will not allow it. The never-ending pain loop in my brain.

Whatever happened to me doesn't define who I am.

It just happened.

Taking charge of our minds and emotions means everything will change, and that can be scary. The core of your identity will be shaken up. It takes an act of courage to look within, see it for what it is, own it, and move on.

I do understand what it feels like to want to be consoled. I understand perfectly. But what I also understand is that no matter what we struggle with, there is always someone out there who has it much worse. Just watch the nightly news, and you'll find story after story (none of which are uplifting) about people who are abused, poor, tired and more screwed up than you. Pain doesn't make you special and it doesn't make me special.

When you reclaim your heart and mind and pull yourself up by your bootstraps, you change your entire outlook. When the day comes you are fed up with yourself, magic can happen: there will be no more room for the lost little girl. She will be replaced with a courageous woman who let go of her story.

Here are four good reasons to consider throwing out your story:

1. Carl Jung put it perfectly: "I am not what happened to me. I am what I choose to become." Telling our story automatically allows you and the other to relive a trauma or drama. It's like spreading poison. Why do you need to be consoled? Does your story define you? Why? Why does what happened to you need to be brought up in the present moment?

2. Living your story emphasizes ego and identity in the wrong places. It allows those dangerous thoughts to creep in: I'm not thin enough, I'm not smart enough, I'm too old, I don't have enough money, I will never get the promotion, he doesn't love me. Over time, you start to believe you are the victim of a horrible set of circumstances, competing with another, thinking your story is nobler. It becomes a sick, competitive game that you play called my hurt is bigger than your hurt. After all, who else could have overcome being fired, losing a child, getting a divorce after twenty-five years, and gaining seventy-five pounds? The story itself makes you special and it creates one-upmanship. It perpetuates the inner victim.

3. Believing your story gets you attention. Oh, you'll get attention—for all the wrong reasons. Did you ever hear someone's story that started with, "Seven years ago, I got divorced..." and you wonder why they are still talking about it? If it's that devastating, seek help with the intention of processing the story differently.

4. Living your story creates perceptions. It's a way to lose all control of how you are perceived by others, especially at work. Now the other party has summed you up and labeled you after you shared your story. They have reached all sorts of conclusions about you, and consequently you are out of control. The truth is that you were looking for attention, misjudged your audience, and it backfires. Sharing personal information at work can be downright dangerous. My husband has a belief that there are no true friends at work, and some days I buy into this theory. Work is a place to showcase skills and earn money. It can get weird if you tell the wrong story to the wrong person. Remember, women bond through pain and suffering; men do not. Tell the wrong story in front of the wrong people in the office could cost you a promotion.

Don't kid yourself. Your story has no value. However, how you quietly came to conclusions about it, how you processed it, has great value. It takes a level of deep commitment to let go of the story and create something good out of something horrific.

You have *total control over your personal interpretation* of what the past means to you. Your personal interpretation of your "story," is one hundred percent your responsibility.

Letting go of your story is a statement of self-love. It says you are much larger than your story.

Love yourself enough to not perpetuate the problems of your life.

Chapter 11

Forget Lean In

I went through a phase about two years ago where I was extremely focused on ego disintegration.

Whatever it took to obliterate my ego, I was in. What motivated me was seeing that my own ongoing issues at work stemmed from me. For years I had been quick to rationalize that the problems were with the people who worked with me or the company culture. In fact, I became a master at dodging the obvious fact that my ego was the issue. As a hard-charging woman, I don't think I'm alone in this trait. Yes, there are some of us who prefer to drive rather than sit in the passenger's seat, and that tendency can get us into trouble. Personally, I found it stalled my career, which didn't make a lot of sense to me. I had plenty of smarts, great business acumen, and lots of time in the saddle. Basically, I should have broken off on my own or been a director at some large company. What held me back was my attitude and how I got along with others. And when I looked close, what I found was my ego.

Let's be clear. Everyone has ego, and a person needs some of it. In its purest form, it's what allows you to know if you are male or female, recognize your parents, know which country you hail from, and a variety of other facts that make you, well, YOU. Ego also causes division and separation, which in extreme situations can cause huge demises such as disagreements, divorce, and even war.

There are two main ego traps that everyone can fall into: the ego of "I do" or the ego of "I know."

The ego of "I do" can show up in a variety of ways. It comes from thinking that you are the do-er, the planner, the woman who always has a list or is "helping" someone. I used the quotes around the word helping intentionally, because I've learned that helping can be a perception, and it automatically sets up someone as the one in need and you as the heroine. It's still ego, nonetheless, packaged in things like charity, church, nonprofits, and other forms. It can also be packaged in the producer, the business person, the get-er-done person.

The ego of "I know" is easy to spot as well. "I know" thinks they have a vast amount of knowledge—book knowledge—on a subject. "I know" can also be full of opinions that aren't based in fact or proven at all. It can appear as someone showcasing information as a subject matter expert at a conference, or a person who refuses to ask questions, or someone who gets all their information online, to reinforce that they know something.

But what does a person really know? Do you know, for certain, how your coworker thinks? Do you know, without a shadow of a doubt, what your boss thinks about you? You think you do, but you don't. It's a judgment, and perhaps not a fact. It's a perception caused by your brain, not a real knowing. Intuition isn't knowledge, either.

After looking at the two main types of ego, I saw where I lived the most, and it's definitely in the Do-er part of the graph. I'm not proud of it. Oh, like everyone else, I have a healthy dose of being the Know-er as well.

The more I looked at my mind, I found that the only thing I did was worry about was work. Frankly, one day I was sick of myself and completely unwilling to go on letting my thoughts go amuck, and continue disrupting my career.

And that day was a very powerful day for me.

That's the day that I looked my own ego straight in the eye. I encourage you to do the same, no matter how scary it feels.

Look hard at yourself. Why aren't you further up in your career? Why are you not an effective leader? Why are you passed over for promotion? Dare I say it, why did you get fired or leave the last job?

Is it everyone else... or is it you?

Examining what is in your mind and the situations that arise is a position of awareness and power. Embrace it, run toward it. See what is there. Sit in the ugly—you won't fall apart.

Some of us women have large egos, thinking we are on top while others strive to keep up with us. Other women have inverted egos—if they look too deeply at themselves and fall into deep pits of despair and loathe themselves. Often, they can't look at themselves critically because it's just too painful.

What I saw in myself is that I could use a shaving of my ego, and I became a very willing participant in that art. Giving something up (like your ego) allows for an opening.

There are many ways to crush an ego. The most effective is to do the things you hate to do -*immediately*.

What I found was there is a lot to be learned from doing what you hate to do, repeatedly. It's doesn't take too long to find resistance in the mind or a strong sense of loathing.

Walk into the conference room for the 9 a.m. meeting. See someone in there you hate to work with?

Perfect.

See someone you don't like at all? Sit next to them and strike up a conversation.

Drive down the street and get stuck in traffic. Feel your body. Feel the thoughts that trigger the resistance and the feeling of despair, knowing you can't get to your next appointment, and there isn't much you can do.

Receive a simple text and get very annoyed.

What you'll find is nearly everything in a simple hour contains something that you will resist or recoil from, and that is called life. Some of us do the things we need to do anyway and grumble, other of us dig in and say, "Enough, I'm not playing. I'm not doing this." I wanted to relate to my mind in a different way.

When I found resistance I asked myself, why do you care so much about all of it, anyway?

Why do you care so much about where you eat or what the last email said?

Asking these questions got me to question my own ego and my relationship with work.

I became so committed to this practice and so nearly obsessed that I would go out of my way to take on something I downright hated just to see where I was at with all of it.

I'm serious. I used to coin this theory as the "I hate you. Let's go to lunch. Seriously. I'll even buy." theory. And, yes, I really did take someone to lunch that I downright hated at work. I sat quietly and I watched with horror how my mind went berserk with judgment, thinking I knew something about them. Not saying much, I ate lunch and saw how my own ego caused such a huge separation that I started to question all my thoughts around everything. And, occasionally, I found that when I took this so-called "hated" person to lunch, I got some new information about them that instantly made me not hate them ever again.

What I learned about my mind is simply this: I don't trust ninety-nine percent of what goes on in my mind—it's a pack of lies.

My mind is good for storing facts, remembering my husband's birthday, or recalling my driving route home. It's a tool; that's it. Everything else that goes on up there is typically static—worries that run endlessly, stories that are told, or problems that will never get solved.

It takes an extremely strong and disciplined person to separate out from the ego of their mind and get comfortable just watching their thoughts, especially "bad" thoughts. You know, the bad ones that give you an electrical charge.

Personally, my fears always stem from the future. It's never about what is going on in the present moment. I manufacture devastating, awful things in my mind that always start with "what-if" scenarios. Vainly I believed that if I could think about all the things that could or might go wrong, I may be able to build a better plan and avoid them. Nice job, mind; you really got that together. Now you are back to the do-er wrapped in a control freak package.

Today if a challenge appears at work, or a strong emotion presents itself, instead of shrinking and recoiling, I realize that is a sure sign that I need to run, run, RUN toward it.

The problem is never outside. It's always how I perceive it. What I have found through this exercise is that there are no problems; my mind creates them.

Let me give an example of how this works. We all have coworkers we don't like, especially us women. We can be especially tough on the other women we work with in the office. Often, we invent our own problems with the other woman in our minds. Try something different. Instead of seething at your desk, invite her to lunch. Go out on a limb. Notice the feelings that rise in you. Don't do anything or say anything. Just *watch.*

Or, volunteer for that project at work that no one wants at work (including you). Do it because you hate it. Do it until you feel like you are smiling and your face will crack, but do it.

Or do the fearful thing. Ask for the raise. Every female client I've had gets knots in their stomach over asking for a raise or asking for a higher salary when they negotiate a new position. I had one client tell me that she doesn't feel like she should be asking for anything. The thought of asking for money made her very uncomfortable. Great, I told her. Sit in that, and see what happens.

Another way to obliterate the ego is just say 'yes' to everything. That worked well for me. I didn't realize how many times in one short day I said "no," and had a laundry list of reasons why "no."

Where does confidence come into play with this theory of letting go of your ego?

Confidence is built over time by doing the things that scare you.

Confidence is built over time by seeing that you didn't die from a situation, but were merely uncomfortable. Confidence is critical as a woman leader, and even more critical is that your team trusts you have it under control.

Do a few exercises that make you feel uncomfortable and you'll gain tolerance. You will feel stable, calm, poised. Notice how many times during one single day you think, "I don't like that" or "I don't like him or her," and know that is your moment of glory.

Seize it. Become the leader who runs toward it. There is no leaning in, ladies. Run toward it. Run towards that person, place or thing that drives you crazy, for there is your biggest teacher.

What you will find is that it will disappear, because it came out of nothing.

Chapter 12

Transformational Leadership

About two years ago I was in a search for a CIO, when I first heard of the term, "transformational leadership." In fact, out of over 200 résumés, 3 of the candidates put those words on their profile, claiming to be exactly that type of leader. One of those candidates was a woman, who made $1.4 million in her last job as a CIO. Honestly, when I read "transformational leader" on their résumés, I rolled my eyes and thought, "Good for you. You read a book."

Transformational leadership isn't new, but it is the hot buzzword around leaders. Often, you'll find cute posts on LinkedIn stating that a leader is about inspiring people, not making demands of them. The content in those posts come from applying transformational leadership, and the more I consider it, I see how women can really get ahead if they adopt this practice. The sheer nature of a woman is to be collaborative and supportive, and frankly, this is our strength and where men fall short. I highly recommend that any woman who is in leadership or considering a leadership role consider this style, because you don't have to change who you are or read a bunch of junk. You'll naturally succeed if you consider the principals and practice them.

The concept of transformational leadership started in 1978, by a guy named James MacGregor Burns. In 1985, Bernard Bass came along and expanded the theory to include the psychological aspects that this type of leader would have to have or develop, and how the followers would feel and ultimately be motivated to follow this type of leader.

My error lay in originally thinking that this type of leadership style is fluffy, but it's not. I originally judged this type of leader as actually being a cheerleader, which couldn't be further from the truth. Yes, transformational leaders should sell and persuade their ideas, but they hold the team to very high standards.

Examine carefully the traits of a transformational leader, and I am sure you'll agree that women can have this wrapped up if they adopt these ideas for leadership.

According to Bass, transformational leadership encompasses several different aspects, including:

Emphasizing intrinsic motivation and positive development of employees by:

- Raising awareness of moral standards
- Highlighting important priorities
- Fostering higher moral maturity in followers
- Creating an ethical climate (share values, high ethical standards)
- Encouraging followers to look beyond self-interests to the common good
- Promoting cooperation and harmony
- Using authentic, consistent means
- Using persuasive appeals based on reason
- Providing individual coaching and mentoring for followers
- Appealing to the ideals of followers

This approach allows employees to feel empowered. Team members are asked their opinions. The leader doesn't have to constantly set the tone, because after the expectations are set, the team will automatically adhere to them, while holding each other accountable. Everyone knows what to do, and the quality of work that is demanded. The team becomes so strong that low performers will leave rather than be fired. This model works great in small teams or in highly matrix organizations, and ironically, if you read enough headlines of business articles, you'll see this is how the American employee would prefer to be treated. Gone are the days of micromanagement, and even the term "management." Today, people want to be inspired at work and feel that they are a part of something greater.

A transformational leader is not limited by perceptions. They change or transform the team's thinking and redirect their thinking to larger goals. In my case, when I lead a team, I took an entire staff meeting and explained to my direct reports why they did their job and how it affected everything in the company including the job market, the stock market, and even the city. I broadened their lens so much that after my inspirational speech that Monday morning, they could not slump back in their chairs and produce mediocre work. They knew it wasn't acceptable. Furthermore, producing half-assed work wasn't acceptable to them anymore either. They woke up and were reminded that yes, they were important and valued, and yes, what they did touched everything.

Transformational leaders inspire and pull wonderful performance out of their direct reports. For years my husband called me the "Why Girl," because I constantly asked, "Why?" It drove him crazy, but it was just how my mind worked as a child and still works today. "Why?" is the pinnacle question of transformational leadership. Ask your people, "Why do we do it this way? Why do you think our department has this perception? Why do you come to work?"

"Why?" awakens the sleeping giant. "Why?" is the spark of innovation. "Why?" is the fire to eliminating waste in a company and moving toward efficiency. "Why?" when asked as a sincere question and not as a demand, can open new ideas and foster teamwork.

Transformational leaders set a model of integrity and fairness. No one is special on the team and everyone has great value. These leaders go in and quickly assess and set clear goals. They bring a marginal team from good to great, and never take credit. The accomplishments stand for themselves in hard data that is reported to their leaders above. Transformational leaders are not "yes" men and women. They have high expectations, but the expectations are reasonable. They know it's a push for the team, but want to put it out there and test if the team will arise to the occasion.

Transformational leaders don't have to like or even love every team member. In fact, I once told my team that I didn't have to like them at all. Instead, I had to work with them. My intention of stating that was to make it clear that competing for my attention would not draw favoritism from me. I worried about that since I led a team of all men, and sometimes my sunny disposition could get misconstrued.

In fact, I didn't like all of them. I was clear that how I felt about them one way or the other personally didn't matter. How I felt about my team members never factored into the equation. I often wonder whether women can really put aside what they like and what they don't like, and just do a job. Years ago, my old boss and I called on a client. When we the left the meeting, she said to me, "I didn't like him." My response was, "I don't have to like him. I have to do a job and take his money. That's it."

Like or dislike my team members, I would always encourage them, especially on their worst days. I must admit, as a woman leader, it was tough to decide when I needed to kick them in the ass or have an open heart and just listen.

One team member was particularly challenging for me. He was an ex-soldier who had just returned from the battlefield. His body and his mind was a mess, and yet I had to lead him and demand that all team members embrace him, no matter how out there he was on any given day. My theory was that if we embraced him, over time he would settle down, and to my utter amazement my theory proved right. He was very misplaced and didn't know where he fit in. He didn't fit in at home, he didn't fit in at work, and he was lost. The war wounds he physically suffered, along with the mental anxiety, only made it worse, but I insisted that we embrace him like a brother.

This wasn't easy. Especially for me, as I tend to have little empathy for someone who can't hold it together. This team member grew on me immeasurably, and I did feel empathy quickly for his situation and how he had bravely served our country. But there were days when I also intuitively picked up that he was trying to manipulate me. If I gave into that, it would ruin my perception as a leader. There were some very tough days with him and with the team and in those moments, I had to make a swift judgment call about how I would react or respond to them, knowing if I made a mistake, it would cost me. For a woman in leadership, one mistake by giving into manipulation can be unrecoverable but it sets up a pattern with you and the other person, and over time it can become the standard. Others on the team will see that and think they can get away with things they shouldn't.

Even low performers deserve recognition, support, and encouragement for a period until you can move them from marginal to great employees. Leadership isn't giving an order or measuring the processes in place; leadership is about bringing someone from good to great. Transformational leaders know how to stir up passion and emotion in their people and sometimes that's all it takes to have a winning team. Sometimes you have to believe in them until they can believe in themselves.

There are many ways to instill belief in others. Recently, I coached a client in leadership and suggested he create a battle cry. Battle cries stir up emotion in people. Battle cries should be simple, quick, and perhaps even funny. This client was launching a product with the word "speed" in it. I told him his battle cry for the manufacturing workers could be "Get 'Er Done" or "We have a need for speed." Put it on T-shirts, hang signs around the plant—whatever is needed to make it a catch phrase was my suggestion. This battle cry reinforced the message and fostered teamwork. Think about it: If you don't care as the leader, why should the team care?

To demonstrate transformational leadership, the leader must have a solid vision, and inspire that vision for the future. As the leader, you've got to know where you are taking them and never lose the vision. I think many leaders fail because they have a lack of vision and prefer to live day to day. They inherit positions and keep the same standards or change a few processes, but few of them have a vision. The vision should always be supported by data, because you have to know where you are to move forward and demonstrate progress. For example, if you run an accounting team, determine how many days it takes to close the books. After you take a leadership role, see if you can close the books one or two days quicker, and still be accurate. Track it each month. Talk to your team about your vision. Set the expectations. Listen to their suggestions. Get feedback about what takes them so much time in the process. Believe it or not, they have all the answers, and that's another faux pas leaders make: they don't ask their team what they think. Support the team when they fall, but keep them moving forward. Over time that becomes the mantra and the standard.

If you aren't good at inspiring others or selling your ideas, get training on that immediately and embrace your weak spot in this area. It's critical for transformational leaders to be charismatic and constantly able to motivate their people. This takes effort on your part. Not every day will be good, and some days you will just want to hide in your office and not engage with the team. Trust me, I've been there. To do this well, it takes a lot of output emotionally. It takes keen discernment (notice I didn't say judgment) to know when to support, when to tell, and when to sell an idea. Too much of any one thing will not produce a solid team.

Do you have a pile of people or do you have a team? Most of us inherit departments full of people. Often, they are not the players we would have chosen or even want on our team but we are stuck with them. As a transformational leader, it's your job to make the team a well-oiled machine.

Most of all, a leader of this caliber must manage the delivery of the vision while building trust-based relationships with her people. If your people are so loyal that they will lie down and die for you, then you know you have the right balance. They have now given you all their skills, heart, soul, and passion, as you have to them. It's an equal exchange, and I can personally attest, it is the most beautiful thing to experience as a female leader. That kind of loyalty cannot be bought by giving them a raise.

Lastly, transformational leaders stimulate the team to think independently. This means you can take a vacation. This means your cell phone isn't constantly going off at all hours of the weekend, with your people asking questions they should know the answers to but are afraid to act.

For me, becoming a transformational leader meant I could bury my father.

The day came when I got a call from hospice stating my father was in Colorado, taking his last breaths and asking for me. Hospice tried to find me for six months when my stepmother would not release any of my information to them, despite my father's pleading. When the young hospice worker finally got a hold of me, she burst into tears out of sheer relief. Within two days I was on a plane and at his bedside.

I'll never forget walking down the hall with my head spinning about the news around my father. I hadn't seen him in seven years and we hadn't spoken, but I knew the right thing to do was to answer his call and go to Colorado. I had to deliver this news to the team and to my boss, and I distinctly remember feeling like I didn't know how to do any of this, and at the same time I felt my bullet-proof nature was cracking. Like it or not, I had to calculate how I would deliver this news to my team. I didn't want pity and I didn't want a lot of attention about it, either. When something hits me hard in the heart, my tendency is to crawl within and try to be alone with it. The news of my father's impending death hit me in such a personal way, I wasn't exactly sure what to say about it. My father was the last family member to die and I was going to be right there in front of him when he died. It was a lot for me to grapple with at the time.

When I told the team, I made it very brief, and I told them the truth. I told them simply that I got a call and my father was dying and I had not seen him in years. This painted the picture that this experience was as foreign as it was difficult for me. Finally, I strongly stated that they needed to hold down the fort. I appointed one of them as lead in my absence, stating they could make a hard call. I asked all of them not for support, but for silence. No calls should come to me and I warned them I would not be checking my email. This trip was off-limits, and it had no room for work questions. I trusted them. Period.

They got it. Some mumbled they were sorry, but that was about it. One had a very serious, sad face which I picked up immediately. His face, which I can still see in my mind had an expression of deep concern for me and my situation.

Intuitively I realized that the team didn't like their leader to hurt. It was like seeing a lion with a thorn in its paw and seeing the lion in pain, crying out. It also scared some of them. If the leader is upset, well, it's a very bad day in the office. My father's death made me more of a person and not just a leader, which, as crappy as it is to say, worked in my favor.

Dad died three days after my arrival. My last memory of him was feeding him vanilla ice cream. He said very little, but when we locked eyes it was clear to me that his mind was all there, although his body was worn out. I was also clear that all the anger and misunderstanding between us over the years was due to the ironic fact that we were so alike. He and I were the scientists. We were the low emotion people, the stoics, and in these last moments there was no room for all of that. He couldn't deny being old and dying, and I couldn't deny my grief. I wasn't sorry he was leaving the body. I was sorry for all the missed opportunities to put our egos aside and just be together. But in these last moments with my dad we did just that. We sat in comfortable silence while he got to the business of dying.

The biggest gift my father gave me was one little sentence, "It couldn't have been easy."

The gift I gave to him was saying, "Dad, you don't have to do this anymore if you don't want. Just let go. It's okay to die."

I meant it. There would be no tears from me visibly while I was at his bedside. It would be cruel to ask him to stay on this earth, tortured in his body, any longer than necessary. I loved him enough to let him go.

The first day I was there, I was trying to get something out of the visit. I was grasping to get that ultimate picture, the one where he looks at me and says he is proud and he is so very sorry for what he did to me over the years. In a moment, I saw how utterly selfish I was and how ironic it was that I wanted one last thing from my father and he wouldn't give it to me. I'd also wanted this scene accompanied by a piano softly playing Hallmark-movie-style music in the background.

That never happened.

What did happen was I knew he was dying and that we would not get these moments back. Once I stopped grasping, I could support that process with love and an open heart.

I write these next words for all the women who had fathers who were such a disappointment that it drove them to huge financial and career success, because you'll get the next few paragraphs. It amazes me how pain and anguish of what one didn't receive as a child can foster such a spark that ignites into a fire of success out of sheer spite. It is amazing how strength is pulled out of a wounded little girl and who she becomes by the disillusionment of her father.

The relationship I had with my father was tumultuous and I use that word intentionally. What I didn't know is that pain made the woman I am today, and for that and for my father, I am eternally grateful. My father was in fact, my greatest teacher.

I am also old enough and wise enough to know that I was at least fifty percent of the problem in the father/daughter relationship, and for that, I'm truly sorry. My ego was entrenched and I was demanding. Mea culpa. Frankly, it's embarrassing, but I didn't know another way to conduct myself as a child or as an adult with my father. My thinking about my father and my judgments consumed me, and for my part in that, we spent our entire lives at odds with each other.

All the anger, disappointment, and fear between us disappeared, as it should, during those last moments impending his death. I pushed my ego aside and gave to him what I could never give him before—compassion, trust of my own heart, and unconditional love. What he did or didn't do to me didn't matter anymore. What I found was he was human, hurting, and leaving the body, as I will someday. Looking at him lying there, I saw myself and could picture my own last breaths. My bone structure, my lack of emotion while in pain, and all the quirks that made up me were in him.

This is not to say my childish, pathetic emotions didn't rise during our visit; they did. I just did a great job of not puking my needs all over my dad as he lay and suffered. I could sit with him, quietly, in the silence and let my selfishness not take over.

What does this have to do with leadership? Everything.

I could not have done that visit while checking email. I was fully present and a full participant in my father leaving his body.

How one shows up in the private moments of their own life determines who you are as a leader as well, and sometimes those hurts and joys can bring a deeper element into your leadership that you never knew was possible.

When I returned to the office, nothing major had transpired, and my initial gut feeling was that maybe the team wasn't being totally truthful with me. I checked around, and no one had heard anything from my department. My absence was not felt, which is what I wanted.

Ultimately, as a leader this is what you want as well. You'll want your team to be independent and not have to take a bunch of calls when they aren't confident to handle something. Many leaders think if they get a bunch of calls they are being informed, and that is just an illusion to make yourself feel important. If they are doing their jobs well, you shouldn't hear from them, and you can focus on what you need to do.

The day I came back from Colorado, a quiet knock came on my door after our staff meeting. The team lead told me how very sorry he was for my loss. He shared with me that the whole team got together and nearly bought me flowers and a card, but they knew what I wanted more than anything was privacy around my emotions during this time, and that flowers may not be the best choice.

When he left, I shut my door and burst into tears.

Privacy was exactly what I had craved, and they knew me well enough to not buy the flowers.

I cried because I had never felt so loved by a pile of people that I could proudly call my team.

Chapter 13

Data Is Your Friend

The hardest transition for any leader is to get clarity around how you are measured. It's not about you any more, rather it's about what you drove the team's accomplishments. Frankly, data is what separates the girls from the women, and what gets you a seat at the table.

Feeling aren't facts and too much focus around situations can be career killers: no one cares about what you feel at the office. The production numbers should speak for themselves and paint the whole picture in a simple business case. Educated guesses or even your past stellar performance as an individual contributor no longer matter. Data tells all about your team's performance, and if you are armed with that, you can go to the mat for them.

On your worst days at the office, you will have to fight for your team.

Within thirty days of taking the reins as a female leader, it's important to understand what standards, if any, are in place. Standards can be your creation or passed down by the enterprise, but it's important to go to every meeting with some data. This proves strong business acumen and, over time, you'll be trusted for objective opinions bound by data.

Although some of you reading this book aren't new to leadership, it may be helpful to review what to measure. Measure *outcomes*, not processes.

For example, you can measure:

- Accident frequency rates (if you are in manufacturing)

- Client satisfaction surveys (both internal clients and external clients), if your department delivers a survey
- Engagement surveys if you are in HR and want to measure your leaders' effectiveness
- Absenteeism rates if you have a low skill, high task staff
- Escalation and error rates if you are in help desk or engineering

Teams want to trust their leaders. Typically, if you have already done the team's job and were promoted into a leadership role, they will have an amount of trust automatically built in. Have you ever reported to someone who didn't know anything about your job? It can be frustrating when a new leader comes in with new ideas and forces implementation without asking the team whether it can be done.

If you have never performed your team's duties, it's good to get a sense of what they do daily. Hold fifteen-minute morning meetings. Walk around. Get a sense for how they work and the quality of their work before you put in a new process.

Ask other departments for their perceptions of your department and carefully go reflect on their feedback. I found this to be extremely valuable when I lead a team. To my surprise, before I inherited my department the team had gotten mixed reviews. Some departments enjoyed working with us, and others despised working with us—for good reason. We dropped the ball. Considering how we were perceived was important to gain credibility, for myself and for the team.

One you set some standards and measure improvements over the next sixty days, consider implementing key performance indicators (KPIs) for your department. Again, if you work for a larger company, they may already have these in place. If they do, review them because they may or may not make sense. Perhaps you can bring some expertise from your last job and offer it to your new company.

Key performance indicators are extremely valuable, because when a KPI is a solid measurement, the leader can determine whether performance has changed over time and keep the team focused on what matters the most to their success. Additionally, KPIs can create a common language for you and the team to see how your vision is coming to fruition.

Since KPIs must be linked closely to the business needs, deciding what to measure is critical. All measurements must be quantifiable and reported as accurately as possible. Consider how you will pull the data carefully before you start implementing KPI standards and measurements. For example, will the software you use automatically pull data weekly? Or do you have to manually track all of it on Excel spreadsheets?

For the first quarter after you implement the standards, carefully watch your team to see whether they are hitting the targets monthly. Ask for feedback to uncover any inefficiencies or ways that you can produce better quality work. Don't assume you have all the answers, but instead leverage the knowledge of the team. Many leaders make this critical mistake. They think they know it all. After all, they were hired out of a pack of candidates to come in and do a good job, and whatever they sold during the interview is what they need to perform to as the new standard. The team knows way more than you could ever know walking in the door. Ask for their input, yet balance your authority. Asking for too much input as a female leader will give them the impression you aren't competent, and leave your team feeling like they can run over you. What I personally found was that asking the team empowered them, but a little too much was bad for how they perceived my ability to lead them.

After creating solid measurements for the team, consider forming team norms. Team norms create unity, bonding, and a shared language that are ultimately relationship guidelines. These rules of engagement outline habits that become behavioral expectations over time. Team members learn to trust each other—not just you—and quickly see they are a part of something bigger than just the daily grind.

It's critical that team norms are created by the team, and not by the leader. The leader's job is to orchestrate the exercise, and nothing more. Establishing team norms can cut down on petty disagreements or political snafus. Although the idea of this may seem too touchy-feely, it isn't. I personally did this exercise with my team of all men, and it worked out very well.

Initially, the team may have a hard time coming up with their rules of engagement, and you might need to throw out one or two to get the creative juices flowing.

Team norms look like this:

- No one speaks over each other during meetings
- We don't throw anyone under the bus
- We are accountable for our work and the quality of our work
- Meetings are a place to discuss problems without attacks or retaliation
- Problems are presented in a way that fosters discussion and resolution by leveraging the team
- No one is the smartest person in the room
- Everyone's contributions matter
- If the team sees a warning sign or anticipates something that is about to go wrong on a project, they should raise the flag immediately
- Knowledge is power, and is shared

Too many team norms can create confusion, so even if you see a few good ones above, allow your team to pick the values most important to them. Jot them all out on a whiteboard and encourage the team to pick three to five of them. The entire team must be in agreement with what is chosen because this is the new code they will live by moving forward.

Print the selected norms out and hang them in the cubicles to remind everyone that they are a part of something larger than just themselves. This exercise can be a lot of fun, and actually be very telling the leader about what is really important to the team. I suggest every team member contribute one team norm so everyone has skin in the game. Don't allow the introvert in the back of the room to avoid contributing during the exercise. Make a point of asking for their input. You might uncover a diamond.

Team norms are adhered to in every situation, every day. When someone doesn't follow the team norm, the team members should feel safe to call the other one out. Behavior is changed over time, so don't be frustrated if you don't see huge change overnight.

Know that it will take the first two quarters at work to establish yourself with the team and with the executives. It's dicey, but careful and strategic thought, rather than just reacting to your day, will pay dividends. Take Friday afternoons, if you can, and just review and think for a half hour. Play back the week and what you accomplished. Think about the interactions you had with you team members individually and in meetings. Consider what you could do better the next week. Schedule this time as it if were an appointment, because it is an appointment—with yourself. Allowing yourself the precious gift of time will slow things down so you are more methodical and not as reactionary.

Meeting with your staff weekly and individually can be a practical way of measuring performance. Have structured one-on-ones with your staff and go over the data. Many direct reports don't know what to say or what to ask for in their one-on-ones. Have an outline for each employee of items you'd like to go over, or reinforce what you said in the staff meeting. I distinctly remember going to one meeting, early in my career, and intuitively knowing my boss had no plan of what to talk about during our meeting and it actually made her uncomfortable to give any feedback. I'm constantly surprised when I work with leaders and ask them about their one on one's with their staff and how few have any planned agenda. Planned meetings sound oversimplified, but are the obvious thing we overlook. Don't expect your direct report to come prepared to the one on one. Few do. It's your job to set the tone and focus.

And finally, as a female leader you want to be approachable to your team. Some female leaders build a wall around their hearts because they are so afraid of being considered too soft or fear of being taken advantage of in the office. Leading with the heart and head is the most powerful attribute a woman can have in a power position. Don't be fearful.

Being approachable is important, and again, for a female, it's a delicate tightrope. The last thing you want is to be manipulative. Being friendly is important, or they will not trust you and come to you when things are going wrong. However, being too friendly can lead to favoritism and possibly manipulation. The entire team should be treated fairly, and not be subjected to your personal judgments. You may not like your direct reports but that shouldn't matter. Look for their value and past their quirks.

Data will eliminate a witch hunt at work. People will make mistakes, but there is no reason to blame a person and make it about them. Look at broken processes, not at people. See if the team member broke the process, and train them. Generally, people don't intentionally make mistakes. No one hits the alarm clock and thinks, "Gee, I think I'll do a bunch of crappy work today." Try not to display anger when a team member really botches something. Ask questions, looking for the link that broke in the chain. Ask until you are satisfied that you got the entire story without making any judgments or assumptions. The safer the team feels with their leader, the more they will disclose when it starts flying around the office.

Leadership is providing a place for people to screw up, as well as be innovative. Leadership sets a tone and a vision, and keeps the team moving toward the goal.

When mistakes are made, and inevitably they will be made, point back to the data. If you have the unpleasant experience of having to fire someone, point to the data. If you constantly point to the data, it's not possible for someone to take things personally. For example, let's say a team member makes a mistake and you let them know. Rather than starting with saying, "We found that you made an error," go over the policy or procedure. Point out the policy or procedure that was broken, and steer clear of blame. What you'll find is that with this approach, people will not take it personally, and ultimately be accountable.

Chapter 14

We Have to Talk

Delivering difficult feedback with grace is one of the hardest things a female leader can do, and is the most necessary skill to master. In general, many women when delivering feedback sound angry, judgmental, or attacking. It could be the tone of their voice or the look on their face, but whatever it is, it's not good. Others can't quite say what they need to say, leaving the team member fuzzy about what really took place in the one-on-one meeting. As I've said before, it's a delicate balance. Delivering negative feedback can be very difficult if this is your first leadership position.

Ultimately, you want to deliver feedback in a way that makes a person grow. It's like gently tapping them on the shoulder and making them aware. The team member feels it, but you didn't bruise them. As women, we struggle with being honest and fear our honesty and transparency will hurt another. What I've found is that it's never my content that gets me in trouble. What gets me in the most trouble is my delivery.

We mistake our truth for THE truth. It's never the truth; it's always our perception about what we think happened. The mind creates its own reasoning and we believe it thinking we have the truth, but it's only the narrow confines of our own minds. It's a mistake to walk into any corrective conversation thinking you have all the facts if you didn't ask any questions prior.

Decades ago, the people on top stuck together in an organization and there was power in numbers. Today, the victim has a strong voice, and I'm honestly not sure either path is good.

For example, someone has a tough day at work, and before you know it, HR is involved and in the end, what really happened was that someone got their feelings hurt in the office. All that was needed was a simple mediation session, not a full-fledged investigation. At the end of the day, this thing called business and the office is derived from people. People who come in and sit at their desks and have full lives outside of the office. Those lives can impact their performance, attitudes, and willingness to connect with another coworker. The crappy part is, as a leader, you deal with that, along with the real business problems like competition, quality of work, time to market, and product margins.

Eventually it all comes back to you, the female leader, and how you navigate through the murky waters called "personality disconnects." It can also be one of your greatest strengths and assets beyond male leaders, if you master the delivery of feedback.

Many articles are out there on delivering feedback, but few talk about intention. The intention of giving the feedback is as critical as the information you are about to deliver. Standing back from what you want to say and considering how it will be taken in by the person you are speaking with is extremely valuable. I think we get very caught up in the words of communication and strive to do it better, but somewhere during the communication we forget there is a person outside of you who is receiving your side of your perception. Women can be at a real disadvantage regarding this, especially if they read a bunch of books about communication.

Sadly, we don't communicate in the spirit of unity; we talk (not communicate) for the sake of being heard, or worse, being right.

Years of self-help books pushed women to stand up for themselves and speak out. What I see is we are screaming all over each other. Even when I watch TV now, that is what I see -

everyone dying to be heard and willing to do something outlandish to get any amount of attention, good or bad. As a society, somewhere we made a wrong turn. There is too much "I" in communication. Little emphasis is on planning what we are about to say and whether it has any value at all.

I found a funny graph online a few months ago, called W.A.I.T., which stood for "Why Am I Talking?" Although I giggled when I read it, the model itself made a lot of sense; I realized that it had to do with speaking in meetings, but could be used anywhere at any time.

The graph included questions you should stop and think about before you speak:

Is what I'm about to say on topic and a contribution?

Do I have very strong feeling about something?

Is this the time to do that?

If so, please be concise.

We get so wrapped up in what we are going to say that we forget there is anyone out there, on the other side of our words. Take time and consider what you said and what kind of impact it had on the individual. Consider the subtle things like the looks on their faces when you spoke or how they held their bodies after you spoke.

Over time, how do you think your communication affects the other person on the other end?

Do you think they tune out or turn off?

Do you think they feel judged or berated?

Do you think they will rise to the occasion and perform better?

How do they perceive you, after your conversation?

Studies show that if you give five pieces of praise and one piece of negative feedback, people will improve. Years ago, I was taught to give people a positive/negative/positive sandwich, or a PNP sandwich. I remember watching a coworker do this with another employee and thinking that will never work. To my utter amazement, it not only worked, but the person turned around their performance immediately.

Today in the office it seems as if there are only two approaches to feedback, and it's a shame. We either point or blame, or we avoid the issues and don't give the feedback.

Many team members may want tough feedback from you. Typically, A players, or those looking for advancement, want feedback to grow and improve. When delivering tough feedback, consider their style of communication to deliver the feedback in a way that it will be taken in, absorbed, and processed. Negative feedback doesn't have to be a negative experience.

Feedback on your performance as a leader can also be a two-way street. Typically, engagement surveys or blind 360 surveys can uncover how it feels to be on the receiving end of performance feedback.

Feedback should always be delivered considering the how and why, not who. Focusing on the who will automatically put the other person in the defensive, and once they are defensive, you've lost the opportunity to have a dialogue that opens the individual for change. Look for body language, small facial expressions, and tone of their voice. The more introverted the team member is, the more closely you should pay attention. It's possible they hear you and are processing what you said, while you may mistake this for a misunderstanding and continue to speak.

Prior to having any constructive feedback conversation, get yourself in check. Ask yourself tough questions; I encourage you to journal prior to holding the conversation. This is the difference between responding and reacting. Respond as the female leader. Never react. Reactions stem from emotions that may not illuminate what is really going on, so before you engage in a tough office conversation or intend to deliver feedback, ask yourself these questions:

- What is the purpose of the meeting with your direct report?
- What are you trying to convey? Can you convey this in less than five minutes?
- Do you have all the information you need, or should you be asking more questions prior to speaking? Is this an information-gathering session or a deliver-feedback session?
- Are you angry/disappointed/confused with the situation? (If so, construct questions and don't deliver any feedback just yet.)
- Are you delivering feedback based on fact, or are you delivering criticism based off of judgment?
- What do you get out of holding the meeting? Is there an electrical charge? (For example, from anger, being right, or pointing the finger at someone's mistake.)
- If this is truly a deliver-feedback meeting, which three points do you need to cover? (Be succinct as possible.)
- Can you deliver this information in five or ten minutes?
- What is the best outcome for both of you?
- Do you intend to have a follow-up conversation to see if the person processed the information and is making changes?

Notice I suggested that you be succinct as possible. If you are succinct, you are delivering information. If you tend to go on, it's likely your feelings, opinions or judgments and your ego is engaged.

If you still have butterflies around having the corrective conversation, consider how your direct employee feels about walking into your office. What kept me the most in check as a leader was thinking about all the times my stomach was sick the day before I had a meeting with my boss, only to find the conversation wasn't nearly as heavy as I anticipated. We've all been there, replaying conversations in our heads or guessing what our boss will say at the 9 a.m. meeting. It's horrible. I remembered what it felt like to fear the boss and know they ultimately had control over my livelihood. I vowed to never let anyone who reported to me to feel the same way. I committed to myself that I would still set boundaries for the team, but never instill fear, knowing that I could be heavy handed. The hardest part for me in leadership was to find out that not everyone understood my standards of excellence. Not everyone jumped out of bed excited to go to work and do something great. By my mid-thirties I was told I was the anomaly, and I had to agree. People go to work to get a paycheck and have money for their families. For me, work was always a magical place with innovation, collaboration, and challenges. Work excited me, and still does.

Consider timing when delivering feedback. Try opening difficult conversations right after the situation occurred in order to pull the best result. Letting the other party hear your voice rather than get an email. While email is easy, it strips out your tone and intention. A voice builds connection and is less scary for the employee.

Consider whether you are delivering feedback to a male or female, because even that can have a subtle impact. Typically, men want the facts with few sentences. Give them the information, provide them an opportunity to digest or talk through their side, and leave them be. Check back in a couple of days and see how they are doing. If there is improvement to be seen, it will happen immediately. At least, that was my experience when I lead a team of men or had to give unpleasant information to an executive.

If you are delivering feedback to a female, be direct but warm. Think about how you like to be treated when you get tough information thrown at you. Have a discussion, not a blame game session. Lead the conversation but allow for dialog if the employee needs to be heard.

Looking back, two of the best bosses I ever had were female. Both were fair, and I distinctly remember that they didn't always favor me out of other team members, but I respected them and their style. Both had the hallmark of asking a lot of questions rather than jumping to conclusions. It made me feel safe to tell them my side of what was going on, without getting defensive or tuning out. Whatever they asked of me I delivered right away. In fact, I dropped whatever I was doing when they asked something of me to show I was responsive, they were important, and I was engaged. Part of my responsiveness came out of their willingness to be transparent and even wrong on some occasions. It was a fair environment and they both pulled the best out of me.

Giving tough feedback will depend on how you are feeling about the subject and the exact words you say to deliver the information.

Focus on being grounded, curious, problem solving, and supportive.

You can never go wrong if you lead with your head and heart.

Chapter 15

Transparent and Authentic Leadership

In 2015, I was invited to give a talk on leadership to women in the Institute for Electrical and Electronics Engineers (IEEE) Photonics Society. All the women who attended the conference had education and PhDs in physics. At the end of my talk, one woman asked me about my thoughts on being a transparent leader. I paused a long time, and answered that being transparent was fine, but if the information that you were about to release would damage or hurt another person, then it's not being transparent; that's something else.

After the discussion, the woman sought me out and complimented me on my speech, and in return I complimented her on the question. Honestly, I had not been asked that before and wondered what drove her to ask the question. She disclosed that she was gay and an engineer, and further explained that studies revealed that holding onto that kind of information can be damaging and impact one's work. She further explained, if someone asked about her weekend, she must think carefully before she responded and be cognizant to use words like "partner" or "friend" when she really meant her lover. She was very clear that being gay in her field could cause biases and even retaliation. After reading several studies, she found that to be transparent around her personal life without shoving it in people's faces was the way to go.

Sexual orientation isn't the only place the transparency issue can arise. I've worked with Muslims who prayed five times a day and did fasts during the year that fell on company holidays, which didn't allow them to participate. At some point, they had to reveal their religious beliefs to move about in the working world. Let's face it: transparency is scary; it means being vulnerable.

Transparency is a touchy subject. My thought is that it's important to be authentic and transparent at work *up to a point*. There is a fine line when you might think you are being transparent, and it's about more about you making a statement to invoke a response, like "I am gay." It's a fine line to disclose something personal about yourself or deliver really bad news about your organization without your opinions about it bleeding through. A leader can be somewhat transparent—human, I guess is how I would phrase it—without tipping the scales.

Personally, I have found that being transparent with work issues (for example, delivering bad company news such as layoffs) is the only way to go, and quickly squashes any rumors that could arise among the team. People talk when they don't have information, and before you know it, you end up with a handful of people whispering in a cube and assuming the worst, which ultimately impacts their performance, because they are so upset they cannot perform.

Americans became emotionally crippled after the 2009 financial fallout. My second book, *I Quit*, was dedicated to the survivors of recession and all they had endured. Just about everyone was laid off or knew someone (or some families) who were adversely impacted by the recession. It was, for most of us, a devastating time. I distinctly remember every night talking about losing either my job or my husband losing his, and the plan we had to escape the west coast and swap the trees and hiking for money and sun in the south. It was a time of whispering in hallways and wondering as you sat at your desk if you were next. Engineers cringed if their products weren't released on time; accountants had long faces as they strolled through the hallways. Everywhere you looked it was grim, except for the transition firms like Drake Beam Morin or Lee Hecht Harrison because they were the only businesses that thrived.

Because of those scars, employees long for trust and transparency. People, Americans especially, want a love affair, not just a job. They look for a job to enable them to feel they are making a difference.

Believe it or not, your team inwardly longs for you to be, above all, a person.

Transparency is a component of the building blocks of vulnerability and trust, the two things that leaders worry about most. How much is too much to tell?

I think part of the reason the recession scarred so many of us is because many of us didn't see it coming and had no financial fallout plan. The recession didn't hit all at once, either. It continued for months, instilling a quiet fear in all of us. Leaders at that time became very quiet around earnings and projections until the numbers came out, and then they laid people off. I knew it was bad when I walked into what were once flourishing businesses, only to find no receptionists at the front desk. Cuts came at the very top, where high-six-figure earners came tumbling down, as well as at the bottom, when all the support staff became a luxury rather than a necessity.

Therefore, people today at work crave transparency.

In 2014, CareerBuilder did a survey with over three thousand employees, asking why people left their jobs, and found that thirty-seven percent left due to a poor opinion of their bosses' performance. (http://www.eremedia.com/tlnt/survey-20-of-workers-say-they-plan-to-change-jobs-this-year/) Lack of transparency can add up to losing staff. *Harvard Business Review* did a similar survey and found that 70 percent of employees were more engaged when senior leadership gave them updates on the

company's financials and progress.
(http://www.entrepreneur.com/article/245461)

Transparency shows up in many ways: it can be a simple as holding weekly meetings and reporting the company's stock value, to articulating clear goals and objectives. It seems like an easy task, but it's not. Consider how many levels of people pass information down to you as the leader and by the time it reaches you, what are you responsible for reporting? When you come in one morning to sixty-three emails, a pile of voicemails, and someone standing in your office doorway, it's difficult to cull through all the information and make sure you are reporting it accurately to your team.

Failure to be transparent comes at a high cost, however.

A survey by leadership training firm Fierce Inc. found that 71% of employees felt their managers did not spend enough time explaining goals, while 50% of respondents to another survey pegged lack of responsibility the number one issue in holding their company back. (http://www.entrepreneur.com/article/232910)

The most powerful exercise I ever did with my team was when I asked them why their jobs were important one Monday morning in a staff meeting. Back then, I planned each staff meeting with a topic, and had a strategy in mind in terms of where I wanted to take them. Sometimes I took them on a training journey, while other times I was planting a seed to get information and feedback from them to eventually solve bigger issues. Monday was never boring for any of us in the large conference room.

I remember the look on their faces and the silence that hung in the air when I demanded an answer. Why were their jobs important?

It took some time, but they shouted out some answers, and I jotted them down on the whiteboard. The next question I asked them was, "Why did you get into this line of work?" Once I understood their drivers, I could see how engaged they were. Some answers were fluff, and I knew it, while others were more thought out. Regardless, I got them to think about what they did every day and the impact it had. Furthermore, I got them to see the impact they also had when they delivered crappy work. This exercise was the beginning of transparency. If I understood what they thought about their jobs, I could then be transparent about my expectations and the companies' expectation.

One of the pitfalls with middle management is they are never trained in how to field questions when they are asked to deliver bad news. In fact, few companies have any leadership training at all for new leaders. If there is any kind of disconnect in the vision between senior leadership and middle management, the divide becomes very large when it comes to transparency. Remember, you are a leader - of a company - so adopting and understanding the vision is important. You'll ultimately end up with two visions: the first is the vision of the company, and the second is the vision for your team.

Becoming a transparent leader is something that takes some practice. Being trustworthy is a good step, and building that trust is as simple as following through. If you say you are going to do something, do it. If an employee has an issue and you said you'd take care of it, get back to them with an answer within two business days. Make their needs your priority.

Transparency also comes from being vulnerable, so if you are wrong or screw up, admit it. The team will not crucify you if you admit to a blunder.

Sharing information is another way of being transparent. This can be accomplished as easy as putting team documents on a SharePoint drive or giving the team weekly updates. Those same updates may also be reemphasized in the individual one-on-one meetings to uncover any questions or issues.

Transparent leadership is a natural fit for women leaders because it allows them to do what they do best, foster relationships. Women can use their social and empathy skills to do what their male counterparts cannot do naturally.

Transparency is the bright light in a dark room that removes fear and creates coloration.

Chapter 16

What Every Woman Should Know

Let's set aside the notion being a female leader for a few moments.

Let's connect with who we are as women—real women. The ones who clean up throw-up, go to work, balance a marriage, get manicures, and worry whether they forgot to turn off their flat irons. We hold many titles outside of work: mother, step mother, wife, friend, daughter, niece, aunt, grandmother. We wear many hats and are expected to wear more if we can. It never ends, and in the pursuit of happiness and trying to make everything perfect for everyone around us, we get lost.

Then the divorce hits at forty-eight, or the layoff at fifty-two; or the child dies; or you watch as your parents suffer and ultimately die. Or whatever...

And we find ourselves ill-equipped to deal with what the natural order of what life dishes up, and we start to wonder how the hell we got so off track. When did we lose sight of ourselves?

We may remember a younger version of ourselves: how she was strong, or perhaps even the unwanted parts of ourselves, like being young and insecure. The shadowy whispers of our fears surface full force when life hands us transition through birth, divorce, menopause, or even the death of a loved one.

I am no stronger to this thing called change and life. I have been there, believe me. I remember one morning reeling through my own divorce and feeling the weight of it. Exiting seventeen years was no easy task, but it was the best decision of my life. One morning I woke up thinking, "Well, I'm breathing. That means I must go on, even if I don't know how to do this thing." "This thing" was about how to be alone and how to be happy with just little old me. Learning to be in my own skin – ALONE – was the most painful and liberating experience of my life.

That's the biggest fear and the biggest illusion of humans: being alone. It's scary, and for women it's devastating. We are built to plan, love, talk, collaborate, and gather.

Being alone is the biggest lie and illusion.

It's in that loneliness that we find the quiet moments of ourselves and if we sit in that long enough, we find we are not alone after all.

But tell a woman who is fifty and just divorced that she might die alone, and you'll see the blood drain out of her face. Tell her she may not remarry, and see sheer terror.

That's when you know you've got a big fat problem: somewhere, you did lose yourself.

As women, we should all know how to do a few things, and mastering these will make us better leaders, but most of all, better women.

Why cry about what is wrong with the world and point outward, when in fact we don't have our own selves together? We do this because, it's easier to work on everyone else around us and frankly, it's hard to be in a constant state of self-improvement.

There is no way to save the world or make an impact without first looking at ourselves, and as women we find ourselves last on the list. Sometimes by choice, sometimes by not paying attention, but for whatever reason, life has a way of throwing a major re-org at you and forcing you to wake up.

I am convinced that life is set up to do just that: throw cold water on our sleeping selves and wake us up.

From my heart to yours, here are some things I think every woman should know:

Every woman should know where her money is at, and have a financial plan. She knows the man isn't the financial plan, and has the great escape money to move out if things go south. She ultimately knows how to take care of herself, and is financially independent. Her money is her freedom chip.

Every woman allows herself some mad money: money that is only for her to spend on a frivolous thing like a new nail polish or a snazzy purse she found on sale.

Every woman should know how to comfortably live alone, even if she doesn't want to. She knows that a man doesn't complete her and can sit in her own stillness on a Friday night, not wondering what she's missing "out there." She doesn't hit forty or fifty and worry about how she cracked up her last marriage and only has so many years to look good. Above all, she knows she is a complete unit.

Every woman should know how to grow old gracefully. She doesn't loathe her old body or her wrinkles. In fact, the older she gets, the more she sees the body as a shell that she will leave behind someday. Instead of hating it, she learns to be with it, peacefully. She knows how to leave her youth behind and step into a confident mature woman.

Every woman should know how to leave a job and do it with grace, not blaming everyone around her as she departs. She owns what she did and didn't accomplish in her last job, and she takes the time to train her successor.

Every woman should know how to love her children, but also work her way out of the job called parenthood so she can reclaim herself in newfound, exciting ways. She doesn't define her children as her own vain accomplishment; instead, she knows they are rented and an exchange, and not things that she owns or did. Her children are hers for a short time, then released into the world. She claims none of their successes and none of their failures because she is not defined by motherhood.

Every woman should know how to be a decent stepparent, if honored enough to be given that title. She doesn't take out her anger with the ex-wife on her stepchildren. She never competes for the love of her husband with his children. Instead, she supports both parents, and still knows her place in the family.

Every woman should know how to use a basic set of tools so she can hang up a picture or conduct simple house repairs if needed. Her ability to be resourceful is her joy.

Every woman should have a dress or suit, along with a fantastic pair of shoes, that makes her feel extremely confident and beautiful, which she can dig out of her closet at a moment's notice for a date or an interview.

Every woman needs to know who her friends are and whom to trust, and which family member to confide in and which ones to keep at arm's length because they squash her dreams.

Every woman needs to know how to comfort herself, and when to reach out because the isolation has become dangerous. She recognizes when her inner thoughts are garbage and polluting her spirit.

Every woman needs that one friend who will tell her the absolute ugly truth and hold nothing back, but do it in such a loving manner she is never offended or angry.

Every woman needs to know how to throw a party to bury the dead or celebrate a wedding.

Every woman should have a home where she is comfortable, where she can have others in her private space for dinner and to foster community.

Every woman should have that one item passed down from her mother, be it a recipe for a homemade stew, a string of pearls, or an old photo that shows her where she came from.

Every woman should know how to forgive her parents and be thankful they gave her life. Despite old childhood disappointments, she makes peace with her past, so her present moment isn't cluttered with pain.

Every woman should find a mentor who is another woman she admires. She should listen to the feedback and not take it personally, and implement her suggestions.

Once a woman masters even just one of the above, then and only then is she qualified for leadership.

It is in this self-mastery that she becomes the embodiment of love.

Acknowledgments

This is always the hardest part of any book for a writer, because there are so many people who helped bring this to fruition, and somehow, I have to sum up all of it in a short page.

For me, this list is precious.

It's hard to say thanks, because I worry the words will not capture how I really feel or the sheer magnitude of what I'm trying to convey. Most of all I worry the words might even cheapen it. Please know as I write these acknowledgments, it's my very best laid out before you.

For Lakshmi: You move in mysterious ways. This is my offering to you. It's all I have and in the grand scheme of things, it's very small.

Thank you for my great teacher, Shankarachaya. I'll do whatever it takes until there is no breath left.

For Ananda Mai, her devotion, love and sacrifice.

For everyone at Sadhana Ashram, who I would do anything for if they ever asked. My love is limitless for all of you. My affiliation with all of you humbles me deeply.

For my husband, who is always there and supported me on the toughest days of my own leadership positions, who listens without judgment and, to this day, whom I admire. I've said it before and I'll say it again: It's an honor to be your wife. You, more than anyone on earth, understand me, and why this is all so important.

For Carolyn Suero, who came back into my life like the rising tide: For you, I am grateful to experience something that resembles family.

For Tripura, and for the friendship and the laughter, especially when it sucks.

For Moon and for all you do for all of us. I have so much love for you, I feel like I could burst.

For Vilma, who didn't feed me cookies and cake, but told me the truth – like a real friend.

For Michelle Adams, who captured me on film and shared her talent with me.

For Sharmaji, allowing me to join in, and to show me unity and love when I was very afraid.

For my doctor, Bina Sharma who reminded me that I am not the body that death will come and not to be afraid.

For my devoted and kind copyeditor, Linda Hwang: We'd never be here without you. No book is birthed without a great editor.

For Trevor Harding, the one that would say... Oh, Elizabeth, can't you just....and I would. You pulled the best out of me and still do. And I don't know how you did it. No one else can or has.

For all the executive men at Fiserv – you know who you are - who coached me and protected me and my game, as I do yours. Loyalty like that doesn't come around every day.

For my old team, you grew me more than words can say. I tried not to stumble around, even when I didn't know what I was doing as a leader. There is no other way to say it: You made me a better person.

Lastly, for all phenomenal women who called me and whom I had the pleasure to coach—too many to list! You were always so much more than clients to me; it was never teacher and student. There was no division, for I learned from you. The exchange was equal.

For Kelle Link and for all we've shared across the pond.

For Sarah Zink and Shivaun Palmer of Plaid For Women. It's a pleasure to be a part of this organization and what it stands for, online and offline.

For Judy Hoberman, who always shares.

For Tanis Cornell of EWF. Those lunches were everything.

To all my readers and thousands of followers on LinkedIn who come from every part of the globe, of every shape, religion, size, and color: Thank you for supporting my work over the years.

The process of writing this book was, and still is, very humbling.

Thank you for everything.

80061749R00081

Made in the USA
Lexington, KY
29 January 2018